Your Towns and Cities in the Great War

Huddersfield

In the Great War

Your Towns and Cities in the Great War

Huddersfield
In the Great War

Vivien Teasdale

Pen & Sword
MILITARY

First published in Great Britain in 2014 by
Pen & Sword Military
An imprint of
Pen & Sword Books Ltd
47 Church Street
Barnsley
South Yorkshire
S70 2AS

ISBN 978 1 78346 356 5

A CIP catalogue record for this book is available from the British Library.

Designed by Chapter & Verse Book Design

Printed and bound in England
By Page Bros, Norwich

Pen & Sword Books Ltd incorporates the Imprints of Pen & Sword Aviation, Pen & Sword Family History, Pen & Sword Maritime, Pen & Sword Military, Pen & Sword Discovery, Pen & Sword Politics, Pen & Sword Atlas, Pen & Sword Archaeology, Wharncliffe Local History, Wharncliffe True Crime, Wharncliffe Transport, Pen & Sword Select, Pen & Sword Military Classics, Leo Cooper, The Praetorian Press, Claymore Press, Remember When, Seaforth Publishing and Frontline Publishing.

For a complete list of Pen & Sword titles please contact
PEN & SWORD BOOKS LIMITED
47 Church Street, Barnsley, South Yorkshire, S70 2AS, England
E-mail: enquiries@pen-and-sword.co.uk
Website: www.pen-and-sword.co.uk

Contents

Acknowledgments

As always many people have helped in finding and/or providing information for this book. All have my grateful thanks, but special acknowledgments go to the following:

West Yorkshire Archive Service in Kirklees and Wakefield for their support and patience in producing resources and suggesting further avenues of research. Other archive staff who were equally helpful include those at the University of Huddersfield, the Brotherton Library, Leeds and at Bury archives. My thanks also to library staff at Huddersfield Local History Library for letting me loose on the Kodak machine.

I very much appreciated the help of Wendy Taylor and Richard Hey of the Huddersfield Light Opera Company for allowing me access to their archives, Melanie Williams for access to the Royds Hall autograph book and John Garside for sharing his extensive knowledge of the activities of local soldiers during the Great War. Pam Cooksey generously provided information and photographs relating to the Woodhead family and Janet Green and Chrystal Roberts shared their family stories as well as photographs. Support also came from the *Huddersfield Examiner* and the Huddersfield and District Family History Society. My thanks also to the staff at Pen & Sword Books Limited who have answered queries and given advice throughout the production of this book.

The author would like to thank the following for their kind permission to reproduce photographs and documents:

Peter Carr, Holmfirth Picturedrome, recruitment poster p18 and 32. A. C. Roberts, Earnshaw brothers p28, Mike Woodhead, medals and photograph of A. L. Woodhead p15 and 16, Janet Green, photo of Gordon Donaldson p48 and 49, William Kenyon, photo outside Denby Dale Auxilliary Hospital p50, Clare Archer and the Blue Cross Society, poster of *War Horse* p63.

The 25" series maps appear with acknowledgement to the Ordnance Survey. Headlines and advertisements on p38, 54, 75, 108 and 119 are from the *Huddersfield Examiner* 1914-19. Those on p11 and 20 are from the *Huddersfield Chronicle* 1914-1916.

The Taylor Library, propaganda poster p90, photo of a Zeppelin III p91, Archduke Ferdinand and his wife p115 and the Lusitania p117.

All other photographs are from the author's collection.

Last, but not least, thanks as always for the support and encouragement of my family.

Chapter One

The beginning

Plaque on the drill hall, Huddersfield

Whilst the news in 1914 was more concerned with the troubles in Ireland, there were still reports about the murmurings and manoeuvrings on the continent. As tension mounted, the government stated that there were no treaties that bound England to fight for any other country – neutrality was a definite option. The *Huddersfield Chronicle* took a slightly different view, commenting that in the event of war Britain would 'strike with the same strong arm and same undivided force which has always made its stroke so potent a factor in European politics'. (HC, 1 August 1914)

On 3 August 1914 one headline in the *Huddersfield Examiner* announced that 'Germany has declared War on Russia', but also commented that 'it is clear there is no obligation [on England] to fight for France if war should break out ...'

The next day England declared war on Germany. Not in order to support France or Russia but because Germany completely ignored Belgium's refusal to allow German troops to march through its country and England had guaranteed Belgium's right to neutrality.

Stranded on the continent

Many people had been accidentally caught up in the war. Huddersfield firms traded all over the world and often had close contact with their European counterparts, especially in Germany. Mrs Sarah Hellowell Carter, of Marsh, had been in Frankfurt staying with her son Edwin, who was there on business, and said on her eventual return that the German military were showing greater activity around the towns and everywhere patriotic songs were being played. The English vice-consul had advised her to leave and she'd immediately gone to Cologne, where there was much confusion with tourists from all over the world trying to escape from the threatened war. Then she'd managed to meet a Thomas Cook's tour, travelled with them in what she described as a cattle truck to the Belgian border and thence to Ostend where she caught a boat home. Even the mayor's family was caught up in the problem. His eldest daughter Emma Blamires was in school in Versailles and she too was forced to leave, being woken at 4 am on a Sunday and not reaching London until midnight after a traumatic journey.

Herbert Brook, a teacher, had an even more exciting time. He'd been in Germany to see a friend, John Falck, another Huddersfield teacher who had won the Martin-Fisher Travelling Scholarship and was working in Cologne. Brook was told to leave the country. Despite all the bridges being guarded and everyone being scrutinised carefully, he began his journey and managed to get to Neuss. He then set off from Cologne on the bank holiday and reached Dolheim, where he and a number of others were 'hustled out of the train and into a large waiting room crowded with German soldiers'. (HE, 18 August 1914) He was advised to walk to the frontier about a mile away, but there he was stopped and ordered back to Dolheim to get a passport from the German commander. He fell in with two Englishmen and a couple of Belgians and together they returned to Munchen Gladbach, where they were arrested. Although the Belgians had passports countersigned by the police they were still taken to prison, but Brook and his companions were advised to walk to Dusseldorf and try to get to Drusberg. They hired a car but were again arrested and the car searched for bombs.

At the British consul in Dusseldorf they met another dozen stranded Englishmen. By this time Brook had only £1 10/- (£1.50) left but paid five shillings (25p) for a passport. Eventually they got to Drusberg and stayed in lodgings, where they were kindly treated by the German landlord. Despite not venturing out on to the streets, they were arrested again and taken to the Oberbergermeister, or lord mayor, who eventually gave them papers to allow them to cross the Dutch frontier into Holland at Emmerich.

On the way there the train was stopped and the men got out. The one who spoke the best German went to ask a German soldier what was happening and, being mistaken for German reserve officers, they were cheered by the German soldiers. Though they had to get out again at Wesel and were treated rather roughly, they eventually reached Arnheim, thence to Utrecht, then Rotterdam and The Hague, where other refugees were congregating, and finally to Harwich and home. Brook admitted he was surprised to have been allowed to leave since Germany had already announced that no French or English between the ages of 16 and 45 were allowed to leave the country, and all the three men were young adults.

Civilian internees

Ruhleben Camp had been set up in a racetrack, using the grandstand buildings to house internees, including any civilians who had been in Germany or on merchant ships at the outbreak of war. Edwin Hellowell Carter, whose mother had had a narrow escape from the country, was taken to Ruhleben near Berlin. Many merchant ships were impounded in the docks and the crews taken to civilian camps.

In December 1914, the mayor, Joseph Blamires, received a postcard from Germany from Barrack No 3, Englanderlager at Ruhleben Spandau internment camp. The Huddersfield inmates, who included William Kemp, James Blackburn, Henry Shaw, Harold Eastwood, J. Douglas Walker, William Clarke, John Dyson and Wilson Cockroft, sent the card to let everyone know they were alive and well, wished all a Happy Christmas and 'a brighter New Year'. The following year a list of prisoners at the camp was obtained which, as well as the lads who sent the postcard, now included three brothers, Harry, Fred and George Emmett, from Rock Villa, Scissett, and G. Crosland, son of Guy Crosland, who was a well-known golfer in the area. The group had got together with many other Yorkshire internees to form their own Yorkshire Society.

They described the conditions as getting better after some intervention from the Foreign Office. The work of improving the conditions in the camp was done by the internees themselves who were, by and large, left to their own devices by the German guards. The British government sent allowances of 5/- (25p) per week to the men there so they had managed to set up shops and businesses, which seemed to be thriving. Gifts from home, however, were not only welcome but needed as food was still in short supply. Whatever the conditions in the camp, at least their families knew they were alive and likely to survive the war.

There seemed to be little difficulty in getting letters back home and details regularly appeared in the newspapers. According to the *Huddersfield Examiner* on 26 August 1915, the men had a lot of time on their hands and so organised various events and businesses. This included a theatre named the *Frivolity* and a newspaper. They also held mock elections, in which the Women's Suffrage party won by a large majority.

In December 1915, John William Dyson was allowed home because of his age – 53. He had been working in Germany for nearly twenty years as a power loom tuner but had been arrested in Silesia before being sent to Ruhleben.

They're here

Almost as soon as war was declared, people were on the lookout for spies and aliens. At Crosland Moor a whole group of spies got off the tram and proceeded to chalk up a 'curious message' on the pavement. (HE, 14 August 1914) A guard was set over this message until the police could arrive, since it was obvious (to the rumour mongers) that these were Germans about to blow up the banks or else poison the local reservoir. It was only later that someone arrived and was able to translate the message, which was written in Esperanto. The group were apparently Dutch and the message was to the rest of the group who were arriving later. Everyone was able to calm down and told to 'keep cool'.

Later in the year all aliens were in fact interned and searches made amongst the many Belgian refugees, just in case there really were spies amongst them.

Britain had had little experience of wars being fought on its own land – for centuries battles had been on the Continent or in distant parts of the empire. In December 1914, the war was suddenly brought home to many people when the Germans bombarded Hartlepool, Scarborough and Whitby. C.H. Crowther, a Huddersfield magistrate and director of Middlemost Brothers Ltd, had been in Scarborough during the shelling and described the damage to the buildings with 'stones flying around'. Others left Scarborough on the earliest available trains, coming to Huddersfield to stay with relatives, and described how the fishing fleet had only just returned to harbour when the bombardment started, leaving many trawlers damaged. (HE, 16 December 1914) The loss of life, particularly that of women and children, was seen as an example of German barbarism and confirmed, for many, the need to fight against them.

Workers' education

On 22 August 1914, the *Huddersfield Chronicle* published a map of Belgium to show everyone where the events were taking place. The Huddersfield Workers' Educational Association set up meetings in the technical college to provide lectures and tutorials of various kinds to help people try to understand the background to the war. There was, they said, a 'need for an educated democracy in order that a proper settlement of the European war might be made possible'. (KC648/1) Other subjects included talks about the various countries involved including Germany, France, Russia and Serbia. Some of the Belgian refugees later gave classes in French and study circles were set up in outlying districts. The empire was not forgotten – Mr Hydari gave a lecture on 'Indian Aspirations', whilst Mr Wilson's talk was about 'Colour and Labour in South Africa'. People were very interested in what was going on in the world and in the changing patterns of society.

MAP OF SEAT OF WAR IN BELGIUM.

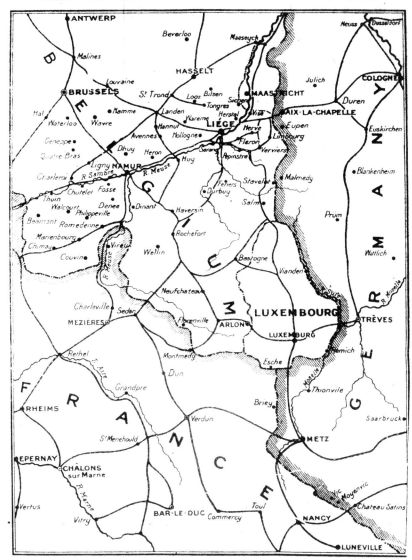

Area of War, Belgium

Throughout the war the town and parish councils had to take on many more jobs, despite the loss of many of their workers to the forces. They became responsible for war relief, war savings, food control, fuel control, providing for the Belgian refugees, and ensuring the correct running of military service tribunals, etc. 'Everybody almost was engaged in sending out comforts to the troops, in organising and serving on Relief Committees of one kind or another. Hospitality was shown to many Belgian refugees and in ways too numerous to mention people were supporting the National Cause.' (E. Lockwood, *Colne Valley Folk*)

Belgian refugees

At the very beginning of the war the Germans had planned to march quickly, taking the French army by surprise and forcing them to surrender in what they hoped would be a repetition of a previous war between those two countries, which Germany had won conclusively. To keep the element of surprise, they chose to attack through the neutral country of Belgium. The German Slieffen Plan was a meticulously worked out timetable of events, specifying the number of days allowed for winning each objective. It didn't, however, take into account the determined resistance of the Belgians, whose tiny army held up the Germans for over a month, attacking supplies and causing delays that gave the British and French time to mobilise their own armies. The German invasion of a neutral country also caused worldwide condemnation from other countries, ensuring greater support for the Allies.

As Germany advanced, the people of Belgium fled. Fleeing first to neutral Holland, many arrived in Britain with nothing but the clothes they had on. Towns all over the country took in the refugees and raised funds to provide them with homes, furniture, food and clothing.

Not just Huddersfield but also the outlying villages undertook to look after the refugees. Cottages or houses were found for families, and each village became responsible for finding at least £1 per week, per family, for food. Flora Lockwood, in her diaries, commented that when the first Belgians arrived in November there was great excitement, with Belgian flags flying to welcome them. They were taken to the Town Hall for tea before going to their accommodation. Most were women and children from Antwerp, whose husbands were fighting in Belgium. One woman had five sons still there.

Two families, Mr and Mrs Peters and their son and Mr and Mrs van Dessel, whose baby girl had died of pneumonia on the journey, went to cottages in Kirkburton, while a further sixty refugees were housed in Royds Hall, which had been cleaned, repaired and equipped by volunteers from Huddersfield.

Many of the refugees told of the great atrocities committed by the Germans and of the bombing of Malines, where hardly a building was left standing. They had had to walk from their homes to Antwerp, then journey through Holland before reaching England and finally Huddersfield. Unfortunately most of them spoke Flemish, so communications were difficult. But a few spoke French and acted as interpreters.

Flora Lockwood noted in her diary that there were many adjustments to make as destitute people came in and had to adjust to a new way of life, while some of their 'hosts' felt that 'they don't seem contented with aught we do for them'. When she went to visit a house that was being used by a number of Belgian families, she found them quite comfortable, with 'some round the fire, some playing cards and smoking and others playing a strident accordion'. But one of the helpers, Mr Lodge, told her that one had said to him 'we like a sausage to us tea'. Mr Lodge returned 'so do we, but we are glad to get it for us dinner and working for it, an all!' (War Diaries of Flora Lockwood)

There were frequent disputes that Flora had to try and sort out, as she was one of the few who spoke French. Later, many of the Belgians found work in local mills and were able to support themselves, though this too sometimes brought occasional snide comments from locals who felt that Belgian men should have been fighting with the Belgian Army to secure the freedom of their own country. On the whole, however, there was great sympathy for the families who had lost so much and funds were always forthcoming to help them, with little presents and fruitcake at Christmas.

The *Huddersfield Examiner* wrote, on 11 December 1914, that 'over three thousand pounds' had already been raised to help the refugees. 'Without making comparison with other towns,' it continued, 'we may heartily congratulate the Huddersfield district on having so freely and generously recognised the claim not of humanity only but of the heroic valour which held the hosts of Germany at bay long enough to enable the stronger Allies to organise an effectual resistance …'

Despite the reasonably harmonious feelings between the Belgians and Brits, not everything went according to plan. In January 1915, Charles Louis Wonters, a Belgian refugee, was in court for being drunk and refusing to leave the Royal Oak Inn, in Paddock, on New Year's Day. As he only spoke Flemish an interpreter, Mr G. P. de Schryvere, had to be brought in. Wonters pleaded guilty, saying how much he regretted his actions and promised never to repeat it. He had no money and had been constantly 'treated' by the people in the area. He was imprisoned until the court had finished its session, though the chairman of the bench expressed his opinion that the man had been more sinned against than sinning and warned that people should beware of 'tactless treating' (HE, 9 January 1915), because foreigners were not used to the strength of English beer.

Later that same year a young Belgian was killed in a road accident. Robert Raymond Felix Duviensart was only 17 and was employed as a dyers' apprentice. He was also studying at the technical college and was on his way there on a bicycle he had borrowed from a workmate. Unfortunately, it only had brakes on the front wheels and when the young man lost control on the bend of a steep hill, he flew over the handlebars straight into a wall. Despite being taken to the infirmary, he never regained consciousness. It was felt, at the inquest, that he was not used to riding bikes on hilly country lanes, only on the flat lands of his home country.

One of the most popular ways of raising money was to hold concerts, such as that at Hillhouse Congregational Church where the choir sang extracts from the National Anthems of the Allies, *Land of Hope and Glory, My Old Shako* and *It's a Long Way to Tipperary*, along with other popular songs. Some of the refugees attended the event and the money raised was donated to the refugee fund. In February 1915, the Belgians themselves were able to give a concert. These included some top singers from the Opera Houses of Brussels, Antwerp and Ostend. Accompanying them was Maurice Dambois, a professor of music at the Liege Conservatoire. Huddersfield was called upon to 'display both their love of good music and their further sympathy with a cause they have already supported splendidly'. (HE, 11 February 1915)

In April 1917 the Belgian Relief Fund officially closed as America took it over.

As the war drew to a close, many wanted to return to their own country, despite the privations they would undoubtedly suffer, and tried to travel to the nearest ports. The government had to explain that repatriation would be done gradually and all would be called as transport and accommodation became available.

Once safely home, some sent letters back, such as that from Malines, from the De Costre family, thanking everyone in Netherton for their kindness: 'To let us live so happy and comfortable. The children are very sorry they had to leave Netherton and think a lot about it. We talk about it every day.'

Another described life in Belgium after the war, with houses blown down by the bombardment, no work, little food. 'We are thanking from the deepest of our hearts for the kindness you have shown us during our stay in your town.' (KC65 Belgian refugees committee)

A letter from Monsieur Anneessens of Antwerp appeared in the *Huddersfield Examiner* describing the bad situation in Belgium and giving 'my kind regards, please, to Mr Woodhead, the newspaper director who worked so much for the relief of Belgium'. (HE, 27 November 1918)

King Albert of Belgium instigated a special medal for those giving humanitarian assistance to Belgians during the war. The King Albert Medal was awarded to Arthur Longden Woodhead for his work in raising funds for the beleaguered people of Belgium.

A L Woodhead

Medal awarded to A L Woodhead

Chapter Two

In and out of the forces

Immediately war was announced, the mobilisation proclamation was posted on the Market Cross where a large crowd quickly gathered round and cheered loudly.

Market Cross, Huddersfield

The local battalion of the Duke of Wellington's West Riding Regiment (the Dukes) was mobilised in Huddersfield as preparations for war began. Prayers for peace were held at churches and chapels in the area but, despite misgivings, 'the scene at Holmfirth drill hall was one of unbounded enthusiasm' (HE, 4 August 1914), as the Holmfirth Territorials received orders to mobilise and join the headquarters.

These are Holme Valley Lads.
Fall in, and join in the ride to Berlin.

Recruiting Poster, property of Holmfirth Picturedrome

On 5 August, the men were paraded and the vicar of Huddersfield, Reverend C. H. Rolls, 'offered a very impressive prayer… large crowds witnessed all the preparation in the vicinity of the drill hall and men with rifles and bayonets drawn were posted at each entrance'. (HE, 5 August 1914) The same newspaper suggested that though the streets were lined with people watching, waiting to say goodbye to their men, they were generally very quiet. As the men marched into St George's Square there was a large crowd, but here again no major demonstration of enthusiasm. However, the *Huddersfield Chronicle* saw things differently. They reported that 'as they entered the station, enthusiastic cheers were raised by the many thousands of people who had assembled in the square'. (HC, 8 August 1914)

Trays of pork pies were sent by a local butcher and Sir William Raynor sent a supply of magazines and newspapers. It would appear that Huddersfield was already showing support for its men but not necessarily for the war. Over 1,000 local Territorials left for Immingham that day with full war kit.

The *Huddersfield Chronicle* also reported on 8 August of the mass meeting held later by the Trades and Labour Council as a protest against the war. One of the leaders made the comment that the war 'threatens to involve the whole continent in an orgy of bloodshed unparalleled in the history of mankind'. He

Sir William Raynor

had no idea how accurate that would prove to be.

Both newspapers reported on all the meetings being held over the next few weeks with stirring language, though *The Worker* was less enthusiastic. It was to write later that, though war could be justified in terms of defending one's right to sovereignty, 'the waste of it and the horror of it remain all the same'. (18 December 1915)

Recruitment Advertisement

THE CALL TO ARMS.

LORD KITCHENER

Calls for 100,000 men for His Majesty's Army and

HUDDERSFIELD

Calls upon its sons to do their duty and provide its share of this force.

THE TERMS OF SERVICE ARE:

1. General Service for the duration of the War.
2. Age for Old Soldiers, 30 to 42. Age for Recruits, 19 to 30.
3. The Families of Married Men who join will receive Separation Allowance.

YOU CAN ENLIST

At the Huddersfield Recruiting Depot, Albany Hall, Clare Hill, the Huddersfield Drill Hall, or the Milnsbridge Drill Hall.

Come and help fill the ranks of the old

DUKE OF WELLINGTON'S OWN.

GOD SAVE THE KING

Drill Hall, Huddersfield

The first meeting at the Town Hall had been packed to capacity, ladies filling the balcony and men streaming into the seats below, long before the time set for the meeting. The organist, A. Pearson, played patriotic songs, with the audience enthusiastically joining in the choruses. Eventually the drill hall had to be opened and more people crowded in to hear the speeches. The following day it was reported that 'Army recruiting has been steady, if not brisk, locally' (HE, 26 August 1914), and after the meeting had actually increased.

Although Huddersfield never raised a Pals brigade, the local battalions comprised mainly men from the area, often friends, relatives and work colleagues, the Dukes 2nd 5th Battalion of 550 men was 'successfully raised in Huddersfield', including men of all ranks. (HE, 1 March 1915)

Soldiers in preparation

Rowland Hely Owen, son of a local solicitor, was in musketry school in Kent when war was declared, joined the 2nd Battalion of the Dukes and wrote from Portobello barracks in Dublin on 9 August that: 'This existence is simply awful – I think I may fairly say that I have tasted of the horrors of war now. Just hanging around, getting things done, sometimes in a great hurry, and generally feeling very fed up and weak.' (KX324 letters of R. H. Owen) Like so many other young men he would soon discover that the 'horrors of war' were still to come.

Huddersfield Military Training Corps were responsible for getting the men ready for posting to the Front. Route marches around the area were held every day, including Christmas Day, partly to get the men fit, but also acting as, it was hoped, a spur to other men to join up. The first of these marches was described as being on roads muddy and full of puddles, but the men remained 'very enthusiastic and full of military ardour'. (HE, 10 December 1914) Groups from all the villages around were doing the same thing and more and more accommodation was needed for drilling, etc. Swedish drill (a form of physical education, rather than military drill) was taught to all the troops. The local battalion of Territorials was also sent to Doncaster for further training. Colonel Thorold, in charge of 33rd Recruiting Area, had much praise for the efforts of the Training Corps.

The 7th (Colne Valley) Reserve Battalion, West Riding Territorials had their HQ in the drill hall in Milnsbridge.

7th Battalion, Duke of Wellington's West Riding Regiment

St Paul's Church, Armitage Bridge

The recruits were all billeted in the area, which became like a 'miniature garrison town' where the streets were 'crowded with khaki clad soldiers learning the serious business of war'. (HE, 3 December 1914)

Although women were not able to join the army and go to fight, they often ended up on the front line through their work in the hospitals.

One example is Sister Ada Stanley, who trained as a nurse in the Royal Infirmary and later worked in Sheffield. She was part of the Territorial Force Nursing Service and was sent on active service to the Dardanelles in July 1915, going out initially on the hospital ship HMS *Northland*. She returned to England with a group of wounded soldiers in October before going to the Near East again on the hospital ship HMS *Aquitania*. In December, she returned to England on HMS *Mauretania*, again escorting wounded soldiers, but unfortunately developed dysentery. She was taken to the military hospital at Netley, near Southampton, where she later died. A memorial service was held in the wooden church at the Base Hospital in Sheffield while her body was returned to Huddersfield for burial in Armitage Bridge, where the bearers of her coffin were soldiers from the local regiment.

Ada Stanley was also the cause of a dispute that resulted in a better definition of what a 'soldier's will' was intended to be. These wills related to instructions written by a soldier 'on active service' where no legal advice was available, and could take the form of letters or simple statements of intent, without witnesses.

When Ada had been ill in October 1915, in London, she had written a letter to her niece, Ada Louise Stanley, saying 'I give you full liberty to deal with my affairs'. (*The Times*, 21 March 1916) She left various bequests to friends, some to her sister, Emma, with the residue to her niece. However, there were ten other siblings, plus two children of a dead brother who took the case to court, saying that the letter was not a proper will.

The case centred on the dates on which Ada had sailed, whether she had had sufficient time to have consulted a solicitor to draw up a will and, if not, could she be considered a 'soldier' on active service.

Since the letter had been written only three days before she received orders to embark for the Near East, she was regarded as being on active service though no-one was quite sure whether she should be regarded at a soldier because she was employed by the War Office, or a sailor because she was about to embark on a ship. The judge, Mr Bargrave Deane, decided it didn't matter either way, and agreed that the letter would stand as a 'privileged will' with the niece as executrix.

Nurse Evelyn Faulder was a daughter of Joseph Faulder, one of the founders of Stothart & Faulder, woollen merchants of Huddersfield, who had a very large warehouse and beautifully appointed offices on the corner of John William Street and Brook Street. She joined the First Aid Nursing Yeomanry (FANY), which provided ambulance support to the Red Cross. She served in the war zone between 1916 and 1919, eventually earning the Military Medal for 'gallantry and conspicuous devotion to duty …' An ammunition dump had been set on fire by enemy bombs and five members of FANY were the only ones available to rescue the wounded.

Coming home

Letters and cards were sent almost every week by soldiers from the Front. Embroidered cards were particularly popular, but it was the letters that told the story.

As early as September 1914, Victor Rayner was writing home to his parents in Paddock that he'd seen his regiment very cut. All of the group he was in had been killed and he and a lance corporal taken prisoner. Although they had to

Embroidered Card from The Great War

surrender all their weapons, they managed to escape and reached a military hospital: 'If I am reported missing, take no notice,' he wrote. (HE, 10 September 1914) Unfortunately, Victor was killed in April 1915.

Corporal Stanley Elliot, son of colliery owner Benjamin Elliott, had enlisted as a despatch rider, taking his own motorcycle with him. On 2 December 1914, the *Huddersfield Examiner* reported his description of his activities as being 'dangerous and difficult'. 'Much of the riding,' he said, 'had to be done at night, more often than not with the lights out and many of the roads were in a shocking condition.' Also highlighted was his 'heroic' part in capturing a German ammunition wagon. Publicising the exploits of the soldiers was felt to be an encouragement to those who had not yet enlisted.

Other letters, such as that from Sergeant Hubert Moodycliffe of Holmfirth, mentioned the receipt of various items families and friends sent to the Front. Thanking his friends for the 'fags' received, he comments, 'the weather here is awfully cold; it is just like being on top of Holme Moss.'

Philip Calverley of Marsh apologised in his letter for the delay in acknowledging receipt of goods sent from Huddersfield. He had, he said, 'been in the trenches for eighty hours during the past week,' but was well and now resting in billets. 'The Huddersfield lot are still together,' he commented, 'although the experience of being under fire is rather terrifying at first, you begin to get used to it.' (HE, 10 February 1915)

Many of the letters seem to have been quite open about the atrocious conditions, so families at home were well aware of how their lads were faring.

The increasing casualty lists, although not specifying the total numbers killed or wounded, gave a good idea what was happening. Private John Herbert Massheder, serving in Gallipoli, wrote to his family in Fartown complaining about frostbite. 'I shall never forget last Saturday night as long as I live ... I will tell you all about it when I come home again. I never want another night like it.' (HE, 22 December 1915) On 27 November, as well as the usual bombardment from the Turks, a massive storm, lasting three days had struck the peninsula. Two hundred and eighty men died and almost 2,000 cases of frostbite and exposure had to be treated in hospital. Not long after this the whole campaign was abandoned.

One of the earliest deaths was that of Charles Alfred Fowle, who died on 13 October 1914. His widow, Alice, told a reporter that she would be 'glad to hear from any of her husband's comrades who know the place at which he was killed and could give details of the way in which he met his death'. (HE, 14 December 1914) Initial notification was done using army form B104-82, giving just the bald facts, followed where possible by a letter from the commanding officer. Though the official letters invariably said that soldiers had 'died instantly', in reality this was merely equivocation.

At the beginning of the war there appeared a number of 'patriotic' evidence from various families. The Lee family of Marsh wrote in June 1915 to the *Huddersfield Examiner* to point out that they had four sons serving in the forces. Stephen and Henry were both in the Dukes, while William and John, who had previously emigrated to Canada, had enlisted overseas and were now in France. The loss of two of these sons was rendered even more poignant by the fact that John had actually died just two weeks before his father wrote to the newspaper, but the news obviously hadn't been received by the family. Stephen rose to the rank of sergeant and received the DCM, but was killed on 7 November 1918, just four days before the armistice.

The following year Fred Shore, a hairdresser in Holmfirth, bragged that all five of his sons had now joined up. The eldest, Harry, was in the Royal Field Artillery but had been wounded and was now at home. Two sons, Fred and Kenneth, were in the Holmfirth Territorials, Herbert was in France with the Army Service Corps while the youngest, Robert, had just enlisted with the Army Service Corps, which had prompted his father to write. Not only that but a nephew, Willie Shore, was also in the Fifth Battalion of the Duke of Wellington's WR Brigade. (HE, 1 September 1915) Letters from two of the sons suggest that not every day was bad. Kenneth wrote that he was in the best of health and enjoying himself. 'Now billeted in a wood and it's like being in heaven without the bullets and shells flying around.'

His brother Fred wrote that he was marching 'in easy stages' and was then 'outside a pretty little village and it is hard to realise there is a war'. (HE, 7 July 1915)

By November the Wright family of Paddock matched this number by declaring that their five sons were also in khaki – the two eldest, Harry and Ernest, in the Royal Engineers, Frank, aged 19, in the Royal Field Artillery whilst the two youngest David, aged 16, and William, who was only 13, were already in the Cadet Corps, ready to volunteer when old enough.

The Gibson family of Primrose Hill had an even greater 'distinction'. Their son Jack was only 15. This 'Primrose Hill Hero' had suffered gas poisoning and been invalided to hospital in Le Havre from where he wrote: 'I wish that I were better or out of it. It is terrible out here. You cannot explain what it is like to see your comrades killed by your side and have to tread over them; it is more like murder than anything else. God knows when it will finish; the sooner the better … it is an honour to you to have a son of fifteen years of age in such a war as this.' (HE, 19 June 1915)

The recruiting officers and medical team seem to have been very lax regarding proof of age. Only later in the war were rules tightened up. Parents were entitled to have their underage sons sent home again, but not all realised this and others genuinely felt that it was 'an honour' and that the boys were doing their duty.

One family described themselves as 'the most unfortunate family in Huddersfield'. (HC, 19 February 1916) At the beginning of the war four brothers had all enlisted. James Gallagher was killed in the Dardanelles, age 38. He had five children. Timothy Gallagher was killed in 1915 in Belgium, leaving a wife and one child. At the time of writing the letter a third brother, John Willie, had been wounded and was in Glasgow hospital, but was later killed in 1918. The writer of the letter was the fourth brother, Bernard Gallagher, who had an artificial eye so had not been accepted into the army. However, he was 'willing to do my best, under the circumstances', so had re-applied six times and eventually been accepted. He appears to have been the only one to survive.

The Earnshaw family of Meltham were luckier. Wilson, who had died in 1895, and his widow Eleanor had three sons. In 1914 Becket, the eldest, was 27. His brother, King, was 20, and the youngest, Frederick Wilson Earnshaw, was just 18. All three joined the Dukes at the beginning of the war and all three came home safely at the end of the war, though Frederick became deaf as a result of the noise of the guns.

Soldiers on leave were obviously given great attention, but not everyone was in the army. The Sea Cadets had been formed in the mid-eighteenth century as a way of providing a livelihood for boys of soldiers and sailors who had been killed or crippled in the Crimean War. Quite a number of men in the area joined the Royal Navy instead of the army.

One was a Marsden lad. Leading Seaman Wilfred Whitehead, born in Marsden in 1890 joined the navy in 1907. He was part of the diving crew on HMS *Kent*, which was in the North Atlantic in the summer of 1914 when the RMS *Empress of Ireland* sank with the loss of over 1,000 lives. An American salvage team was

The Earnshaw Brothers: King, Frederick W, Beckett

sent to try to recover the mails and other valuables, but one of the divers got into trouble in the freezing waters of the St Lawrence River. Whitehead was the diver sent down to try to help. He eventually found the man and recovered him to the surface, but unfortunately the American later died.

Whitehead's exploits were lauded in the *Huddersfield Examiner* as an example to other young men. The Marsden boy had gained promotion, becoming leading seaman, seaman gunner and a qualified diver. By 1915 he was on HMS Essex as part of the fleet protecting the trade routes in the Atlantic. (HE, 10 March 1915)

Jingoism or conscientious objector?

The outbreak of war caused considerable tension between those who supported events and those who did not. The majority of the objectors seem to have belonged to, or been influenced by, various socialist organisations such as the Labour Party. Divisions within the groups quickly showed.

The *Huddersfield Examiner* praised the 'practical unanimity with which all parties have agreed to sink their differences in a common desire to serve the state', and derided those who 'querulously complain that its leaders are betraying their trust'. (5 January 1915) Belief seems to have been split between those who felt that the war had been engineered by capitalist and political elite in which workmen had no part, and those who felt that Germany had to be stopped at all costs. At a meeting of the General Union of Textile Workers the general secretary, Allen Gee, commented that workers were in ignorance of the real causes of the war but that barely a year previously workers from Germany, Austria, France, Holland and England were fraternising together at a conference in Blackpool, where all had objected to the vast sums of money spent by each government on armaments. 'And yet, almost before some of the delegates could reach their homes, a deadly conflict had commenced.' (HE, 8 February 1915) Gee's feeling was that the workers themselves would not have chosen to fight a war for which they would inevitably have to pay, both in terms of blood and money.

Others suggested that even working at home could be a form of patriotism. Germany had led the world in the production of dyes and in chemistry. Now it was impossible to get dyes from Germany so the British had to learn to develop their own and build up industries that had so far been monopolised by Germany.

Not everyone agreed. Letters in both newspapers suggested that those who were physically able to enlist should do so. One correspondent commented: 'It ought to be possible not only to make it unpleasant for a man to be a coward, but also to make it unremunerative.' (HC, 5 September 1914) Another described 'loafers' reeling about the streets drunk. 'In a conscription country, they'd be compelled to do their duty.' (HC, 26 September 1914)

However, there was some sympathy for the unenlisted men. After a football match at Fartown, a letter in the *Huddersfield Chronicle* pointed out that in the area set aside for wounded soldiers there was a number from the Dukes as well as a dozen Canadians. Gifts of cigarettes were freely handed to the Canadians, but none to the local lads. 'Is it any wonder,' the correspondent asked, 'that we cannot get recruits for local battalions when the men who have done their bit were treated in this fashion?' (HC, 9 October 1915) The comment from 'Old Volunteer', a *Huddersfield Chronicle* journalist, was that as the letter 'had not yet been refuted' there must be some truth in it and that it was well-known that the local Territorials were not acclaimed as others were, some even asked if they'd been 'near the firing line yet', despite numbers already appearing as wounded or killed in action.

Philip Snowden, a well-known Labour Party supporter who was very much against the war, came to Holmfirth to speak about peace. A group of men, in uniform, tried to break up the meeting but were soundly beaten and ejected by the audience. The chairman of the meeting, G. Boothroyd, commented that he was surprised at this happening in Huddersfield 'where they prided themselves on their tolerance'. This appears to be true as there is little in any of the local newspapers about attacks on conscientious objectors or on those with German names, even after the sinking of HMS *Lusitania*, as there was in many other towns and cities.

National registration and the Derby Scheme

Early in 1915 it was realised that recruitment was dropping, nationally, to only 100,000 men per month, which was insufficient to allow Britain to fulfil its obligations to its Allies. In May the enlistment age was raised from 38 to 40, but this did little to increase numbers. In July the National Registration Act was passed, under which all men and women between the ages of 15 and 65 had to register, giving full details of their employment as well. This enabled the government to see how many men were potentially available together with how many were likely to be in occupations essential to the country, such as producing dyes or farming. In September the results showed that there were millions of men who had not enlisted, were not in special occupations, and nor were they in the Territorials or Special Reserve.

In early May there was a conference of Huddersfield tradesmen in the Town Hall chaired by the mayor, Alderman Joseph Blamires, to discuss how they could 'readjust the conditions of employment in connection with shops and similar businesses so as to release a larger number of men of military age for voluntary service with the colours'. (HE, 5 May 1915) The unions were very much against this. When Walter Sykes of Zetland Mills discharged men on the grounds of 'slackening trade', this was not believed. All the men happened to be of military age and the firm had promised to try to find work if they were rejected by the military. (The Worker, 13 November 1915)

St George's Square

A different approach was to have military parades. On Saturday 8 May 1915, there was a massive demonstration that began with troops coming from different directions. Those from Marsden marched to St Thomas Road recreation ground; from Elland they marched to Greenhead Park; from Brighouse to Norman Park in Birkby; and from Mirfield the troops marched to Leeds Road football ground. All had military bands leading them as they marched through the town and congregated in St George's Square.

Over 6,000 troops took part in that exhibition, while in July the military display took the form of the 168th (Huddersfield) Brigade of the Royal Field Artillery, performing various drills and flag signalling as well as showing off their new 18-pounder gun. Four thousand people were said to have been there, frequently applauding the men and the band of the Huddersfield Volunteer Corps, which played throughout the evening. Everyone was beginning to realise that voluntary recruitment had to be made to work or conscription would be brought in. Recruitment did, in fact, increase in the weeks after demonstrations such as these, but quickly tailed off again.

Another ploy to increase recruiting was to put on show a German gun, captured by the 7th Division during the battle of Loos. Though large crowds went to look at it, it seems to have had little effect on enlistment.

Recruitment was not helped by the attitude of some employers. An employee of the Huddersfield Industrial Society, who had worked for them as a motor-driver for over ten years, asked to be released to enlist. This was agreed and he was accepted into the army. It was only then that his employers told him they would not hold his job open but might find some employment for him in the stables, which would have been a much lower paid job. The *Huddersfield Examiner* was quite scathing about this attitude, suggesting the co-operative should 'take the lead in generous treatment of any employees who wish to enlist'. (HE, 26 February 1915)

THINK!

ARE YOU CONTENT FOR
HIM TO FIGHT FOR YOU

WON'T YOU DO YOUR BIT

WE SHALL WIN
BUT YOU MUST HELP

JOIN TO-DAY

Apply, RECRUITING OF
ALBANY HALL

Recruitment Poster, property of Holmfirth Picturedrome

CE
UDDERSFIELD.

The Worker was already, in 1915, reporting on anti-conscription meetings. Venues for such meetings appear to have been hard to find in Huddersfield, as the largest halls refused to allow them. After being refused at the Victoria Hall, the Temperance Hall and the Fitzwilliam St Unitarian School, one such meeting was held in the Friendly and Trades Hall. No other newspaper attended the meeting and it was reported only in *The Worker*. Those present were described as 'enthusiastic', and it was pointed out that there was no disruption at the meeting.

Lord Derby devised a scheme, officially known as the Group Scheme but usually referred to as the Derby Scheme, whereby men could 'attest' to their willingness to enlist when needed. Any man between the age of 18 and 40 could still enlist immediately, but could also register to show their willingness to go when called up. Officially this voluntary enlistment was only going to last until the end of the year, though eventually had to be extended.

The attested men were put into groups according to their age, with each group being called up at a later date. The men were given grey armbands with a red crown on to show that they had attested and were therefore not shirking their duty. The Huddersfield Volunteer Corps offered to have the Derby recruits come and train with them, at no cost, so they could get in better shape and begin training, which would be invaluable when they were eventually called up. The training was always done in the evenings or on Saturdays, so would not be too inconvenient.

While the Derby scheme recruited over 2,000,000 men, it was still insufficient. The government was forced to renege on promises not to bring in any form of compulsion and required all single men aged 19 to 40 to attest their willingness to serve. The Military Service Act was passed in January 1916, with exemptions for those in important military work, conscientious objectors, religious ministers and those declared medically unfit.

This compulsion was extended to married men in the summer, which caused considerable outcry. Many single, unattested men had taken up jobs in munitions, which meant they could stay at home, earning an excellent wage with few outgoings. Married men had a home to keep which, they felt, would be impossible on a soldier's pay. Faced with the possibility of losing their home and their families being broken up, they organised a protest meeting in the Town Hall. The National Union of Attested Married Men held meetings around the country and insisted that the government should provide greater financial protection to the families as well as introducing general service for all men.

Tribunals

As the attested men began to be called up, local tribunals began to hear the cases for postponement or exemption. In December 1915, they published some details to help those applying. Applications that could be considered included:

Men employed in certain specified occupations, production, transport of munitions, on railways or in agriculture.

'Indispensables' who could not be spared by the employer, provided they had already attested. The employer had to show how the man was indispensable, that he tried to find a replacement and that the work was supporting the war in some way.

Men requiring further time to discharge some obligation or responsibility.

Local tribunals heard a wide variety of excuses. One film maker wanted to be excused on the grounds that the government would lose his taxes if he went in the army, whilst a toffee manufacturer who supplied a chocolate maker said that his going to war would mean the loss of jobs for ten women. Both applications were refused – the toffee maker being told 'not to eat chocolate during the war'. One mill owner tried to get exemption for three of his workers – one fettler, whose job was a reserved occupation, a teaser and a yarn man, neither of whose jobs were reserved. Not surprisingly only the teaser was allowed exemption but the military representative at the tribunal did point out that the mill owner had two sons, both of military age, neither of whom was in the forces. No explanation of this was given.

Many farmers appeared asking for exemption for their workers. It was beginning to be realised that there may be food shortages and farmers were being asked to produce more yet their labourers were also being called up. Often the labourers were family members, so families had to make the hard decision themselves as to which of their sons should go. Other claimants of small businesses were often given barely one month's grace to sell their business at whatever they could get before having to enlist, causing great hardship to their families and, ultimately, the loss of their status as self-employed as well as a business that may have been in the family for many years.

In addition to objections on work grounds, many men were, or claimed to be, conscientious objectors. Those who could prove their beliefs were genuine were treated as fairly as possible. Some were exempted completely, others had conditional exemptions imposed, such as having to spend time looking after wounded soldiers or finding relevant war work. Some were assigned to non-combatant units like the Royal Army Medical Corps. Other claimants were obviously 'trying it on', as they had no affiliation to any religious or socialist group and they received short shrift.

One man was asked 'Are you a conscientious objector?'

'No,' he replied.

'But you said you were when you came before the advisory committee.'

'You refused it, so I gave that up!'

Needless to say, his claim was refused. (HE, 20 March 1916)

Another man was a bricklayer and also claimed to be a member of the No Conscription fellowship, therefore he was a conscientious objector and shouldn't have to join the forces. However, when questioned about his job, it transpired that he was working on a new factory for high explosives. The tribunal declared that as he obviously had 'no conscience' about that, he could go and fight.

Letters appeared in the *Huddersfield Examiner* giving little sympathy to men who, it was felt, 'stayed at home, protected by the laws and army and navy of his country … making money, while another young man must risk life and limb in defence of all that is dear to us'. (HE, 9 February 1916) Letters from the Front showed even less sympathy for those who remained behind, suggesting 'they should get to another country where they would not be receiving the protection of others' (HE, 28 March 1916), though there seems to have been little violence against the men in Huddersfield itself.

Probably the most controversial tribunal case was that of Arthur Gardiner, a member of the British Socialist party. His hearing was accompanied by a large crowd who persisted in cheering him and making such noise the chairman of the tribunal announced that the room would be cleared and the case heard in private. This caused even more uproar, though Gardiner was willing to do so as long as his witnesses could remain. The crowd sneered and goaded the chairman to 'make everyone be as quiet as mice' (HC, 25 March 1916), but it was eventually Gardiner himself who appealed to the crowd to be quiet and allow the tribunal to go ahead. He made a good case for his objections, the tribunal agreed that he was a conscientious objector, but then refused exemption except for two months. *The Worker* was scathing in their condemnation of the tribunal's attitude. 'Did ever one see such a contradiction in terms?' it asked.

Where certificates of exemption were given, the men were expected to drill with the local volunteers, especially since it was becoming obvious that conscription would eventually be brought in. This was not, it appears, just a pretence. The Tribunals kept a check on whether the men actually turned up for drill and where they didn't, action was taken. In Honley, forty-eight men were sent warnings that unless they complied with the conditions, the exemption would be withdrawn and they would be handed over to the military. (HE, 10 July, 1916)

Conscription or volunteer?

It was becoming obvious that relying on volunteers for the army was insufficient. One poet, known only as JWT, wrote in the *Huddersfield Chronicle* on 12 February 1916:

To Non-Conscriptionists
Before the cloud breaks overhead
And the storm draws near
Awake, o ye sons of Britain
And volunteer.
For the love of King and country
For the love of all that's dear
Arise and do your duty
And volunteer.

Don't say you'll go when you are fetched
That were a coward's plea
The slave who toiled in fetters bent
Claimed as great a liberty
Just think your country needs your help
And give it with good cheer
The way to kill conscription is
To volunteer.

The shirker loves his pleasure best
The slacker loves his beer
The knave lets others fight for him
And stops at home to sneer.
So rise, ye sons of Britain
You've nought but God to fear.
Despise the knave and shirker –
Brave volunteer.

Shortly after this, in May, a No Conscription meeting was held in St George's Square. *The Huddersfield Chronicle* was particularly scathing of the behaviour of the speakers and described the 'disgraceful incident' of Joseph Flanders, who got up on the platform and burnt his call-up papers. The speakers were opposed to 'all forms of conscription' but they were constantly interrupted by hecklers, who appeared to be mainly soldiers. (HC, 6 May 1916)

In 1917 the call-up age was raised to 42. Later 18-year olds were called up but, officially, not sent to the Front until they were 19. Even some miners, a

G. R.

Your
King & Country
need another
100,000 MEN.

IN the present grave national emergency another 100,000 men are needed at once to rally round the Flag and add to the ranks of our New Armies.

Terms of Service.

Extension of Age Limit. **Height Reduced to Normal Standard.**

Age on enlistment 19 to 38. Ex-Soldiers up to 45. Minimum height 5 ft. 3 ins. ; chest 34½ ins. Must be medically fit. General Service for the War.

Men enlisting for the duration of the War will be able to claim their discharge, with all convenient speed, at the conclusion of the War.

Pay at Army Rates.

Married men or Widowers with Children will be accepted, and if at the time of enlistment a recruit signs the necessary form, Separation Allowance under Army conditions is issuable at once to the wife and in certain circumstances to other dependents.

Pamphlet, with full details, from any Post Office.

How to Join.

Men wishing to join should apply in person at any Military Barrack or at any Recruiting Office. The address of the latter can be obtained from Post Offices or Labour Exchanges.

God Save the King.

Recruitment advertisement

reserved occupation, could be called up – usually those whose time-keeping or work was deemed not good enough. All employers who employed more than one man had to keep a list of their workers. This included households with servants. By January 1918, changes had been made to cancel previously granted exemptions for reserved occupations if needed and to re-examine other men who had exemptions on health grounds. A few months later, the age limits were again changed, this time to men between 17 and 51.

Chapter Three

Supporting the war effort

Funding the war

As the government needed to raise funds, the war loan scheme was developed. The first issue was in November 1914 and raised £350 million. In June 1915, a second round of bonds was issued. In Shepley, the local postmaster, Mr Brook, held a meeting to explain to his audience how the bonds worked and 'the various methods which were available to different classes of people …' recommending it to anyone who had a little money to spare as there was 'no commission or other fancy charges to pay'. (HE, 1 July 1915) In Holmfirth the unionist agent, Mr H. Gibson, saw that this could help working people to gain more from their savings and that when the war was over and the money repaid the interest would not 'flow into comparatively few hands', but be spread amongst a greater number of people. Some individuals in Huddersfield invested huge sums of up to £20,000, but many were just £10 or so. They could invest through stockbrokers but also through building societies or banks.

Entertainment tax

In 1916 the Budget imposed other taxes, including on a variety of entertainments such as football, theatre and cinema tickets. Duties were added to sugar, matches, cocoa and coffee. The licence fee on cars was doubled for any up to 16hp, while those over that were trebled. On top of that, income tax was increased from 6 per cent to 30 per cent by 1918. The income allowance before surtax was reduced from £5,000 to £2,000. Excess profits tax increased to 60 per cent, and eventually rose to 80 per cent.

The local people were still able to see the funny side of life. The *Huddersfield Chronicle* regularly printed a section entitled *In lighter vein*. On 22 April, after the Budget, the comments were that 'There is much to be said for the Budget – by its tax on matches, it will reduce the number of strikes in this country'. Another line suggested that 'the tax on coffee is probably made on good grounds'.

War savings certificates

These were valued at £1, but could be bought for 15/6d (77p). Children and adults were encouraged to save up for these and some schools operated as a 'school bank' to help. *The Times* held up Huddersfield's War Savings Committee as a good example when they issued special cards to the children in the area. A local (unnamed) gentleman even offered to add the last stamp for every child who saved thirty stamps themselves. (*The Times*, 11 September 1917)

The war savings song

> Sing a song of sixpence, not for nuts and wine
> But to help our fighting men, all along the line.
> Sing a song of sixpence, turn your pockets out,
> Money makes the mare to go and puts the foe to rout
> Sing a song of sixpence, can't you hear the call
> Come and save the fatherland, while your comrades fall
> Sing a song of sixpence, show them British gut
> Roll along the nimble coin, and do your little bit.
> Sing a song of sixpence, for thirty-one you'll get
> The state to certify you hold a share of British debt.
> Sing a song of sixpence, a pocketful will buy
> Of very useful cartridges, a very good supply.
> Sing a song of sixpence, help this simple plan
> Some are giving up their lives, give up all you can
> Sing a song of sixpence, lending to the State
> For thirty-one of them you'll have a pound certificate
> Sing a song of sixpence, push the job along,
> Then when Victory is won, you'll sing a nobler song.

Frederick Warren (HE, 6 February 1917)

Tank banks

The first tanks started to be used in early 1916, though they were not very efficient. A 'tank film' was shown in cinemas at the beginning of 1917, showing the tanks in action at the Battle of Ancres. 'The ardent optimism and heroism of the men is what strikes one most,' stated The *Huddersfield Examiner*, but they also pointed out that the reader's own imagination must 'supply the misery of the mud, excitement of noise and smoke and nausea of much blood and pain'. (HE, 20 February 1917)

Tanks could also be used to encourage further savings, in the form of tank

The Old Palace Theatre

banks. A number of tanks were taken around the country and savings certificates were then sold to the people coming to inspect the new weaponry. The tank named 'Nelson' visited Huddersfield in February 1918 and toured the area. There were meetings at factories and even a concert in the Palace Theatre to push people into investing their money during Tank Week.

There was also a national competition to see which town could raise the most money, with a view to actually being given one of the tanks. Huddersfield's contribution was more than £2,000,000, exceeded only by West Hartlepool, a much bigger city.

During that week there was also an air display by two planes from Lincolnshire, one of which was flown by a Golcar officer, Second-Lieutenant Edward Haigh. They landed at Botham Hall Farm, which was the only space available. The pilots showed off with spinning and rolling, flying low over St George's Square, looping the loop and finally dropping leaflets about war savings certificates over the crowd below.

The Huddersfield plane

Towns and organisations were also encouraged to fund actual weaponry. The Huddersfield Chamber of Commerce was able to raise £2,000 from its members, which it presented to Canada in order to provide a Sopwith Camel aeroplane. The plane, inscribed with the name of Huddersfield, was later presented in a ceremony in Greenhead Park. Despite the rain a large crowd attended to see the event. Among the VIPs were the High Commissioner of Canada and the parliamentary undersecretary of state for the Air Council, who were treated to a 'rationed luncheon' at the Town Hall. (HE, 11 February 1918)

War hospitals

At the start no one considered bombs dropping on an inland town, so the main preparations were focused on providing relief for families, ensuring that jobs continued to be done and planning for the reception of wounded soldiers.

It was fully expected that the war would be of short duration, but it was soon

Colonel Charles Brook had offered his home, Durkar Roods, as an auxiliary hospital.

realised that just one ward in the main hospital would not be sufficient. The St John's Ambulance association set up a rest room at the railway station with three beds, first aid appliances and staff there daily to help the wounded when they first arrived. Huddersfield Auto Club called on its members to volunteer the use of their cars to ferry the wounded to hospital. By the end of October the first contingent arrived – 100 wounded soldiers on an ambulance train from Southampton, many casualties of the recent battle at La Bassée in northern France.

Miss Wrigley became matron there, together with a small staff of trained nurses. Other friends and volunteers provided beds and T. J. Hirst, the administrator, equipped it at his own expense. Thirty soldiers were soon installed. At Christmas 1914, they were treated to a meal including turkey, ham and plum pudding. Around the large Christmas tree were gifts for each one. The king sent cigarette cases inscribed 'Good Luck for a brave man', from Queen Alexandra a box of cigarettes, from Queen Mary a Christmas card and chocolates from Messrs Cadbury & Co. (HE, 30 December 1914) All the food and extra gifts were the result of funds raised locally.

Ten of the wounded were sent to Miss Johnson's Nursing Home on Trinity Street and five to Mrs Taylor's Surgical Home on Bradley Lane. The remaining fifty-five, who were more badly wounded, went to the infirmary. Gifts, such as cigarettes, fruit, flowers, books, newspapers and walking sticks, were supplied too.

Each town took pride in providing the best possible care for the soldiers, even though most had no connection with the place they were sent to for treatment. But the townsfolk knew that somewhere their own lads would be receiving just such care from strangers too. Occasionally, though, there was a local connection. Private John Duckworth, aged 35, had been a railway porter in Huddersfield before the war, living in Lockwood Scar with his wife, Emily. In December 1914, Emily received a telegram asking that she meet her husband at the railway station. Once there the woman walked down the train, holding up their little girl, Lily, who was just 3, so that she could look at her daddy through the window. Duckworth had been injured at Bethune in France by an exploding shell. His left leg was broken and eventually had to be amputated, and his right thigh was fractured, which must have been doubly difficult for a man who was a keen football player.

Voluntary Aid Detachment (VAD)

After the South African war, the government realised that there were insufficient nurses to cope in the event of another war. Women were encouraged to learn basic nursing skills, trained by the Red Cross, to provide extra nursing support to the Territorial Forces Medical Service. Later the St John's Ambulance Corps also trained their own VADs. When war broke out, many VADs volunteered for service. Initially the women worked in this country, but they were also needed at the Front, where they worked alongside fully qualified nurses, drove ambulances or acted as hospital cooks, clerks and cleaners. Many of the nurses who worked in the auxiliary hospitals in Huddersfield were VADs.

One local VAD was also the recipient of yet more generosity by T. Julius Hirst, who had already paid to equip Durkar Roods for wounded soldiers. He presented four stretcher ambulances 'of a type which has been largely used at the Front' (HE, 2 July 1915), so that wounded soldiers arriving in Huddersfield could be transported from the railway station to the various hospitals in more comfort.

Red Cross awards were later made to nurses M. Story and Jeannie Strickland,

Royds Hall

who were both VAD nurses at the Huddersfield war hospital.

Huddersfield war hospital

Despite having space at the Huddersfield Royal Infirmary, together with auxiliary hospitals at Durkar Roods, Trinity Street, Bradley Lane, Kirkburton and Fixby, more was needed. Initially various schools were inspected with a view to converting one of their buildings, but eventually it was decided that the house and grounds of Royds Hall (which had previously housed the Belgian refugees) was most suitable. The borough decided that Huddersfield would raise funds of up to £30,000 to build and equip a full military hospital.

A grand patriotic concert held in the Town Hall in July 1915, with all proceeds going towards forming a military hospital in Huddersfield for wounded soldiers. There were many stirring war songs, such as the *Song of the Vikings* by Eaton Faning for a four-part chorus, *The Army of the Dead* by O'Connor Morris and *When the King Went Forth to War* by Feodor Koenemann. The navy was celebrated with *Songs of the Fleet* and a selection of Russian folk songs showed support for the Allies. (Programme of Glee & Madrigal Society)

Within five weeks £21,000 had been raised and by October the mayoress, Mary Blamires, was asked to perform the Ceremony of Opening – a great compliment to the women of Huddersfield. They seem to have been the organisational force behind getting everyone involved in fundraising, providing equipment and accessories such as bed linen, and even getting children to take part in processions, etc. Over 24,000 articles had been supplied to the hospital

Sketch of Nurse Cook, Royds Hall autograph book

Sketch from Royds Hall autograph book

before it opened and the women were now embarking on producing uniforms for the nurses and pillows, with cases, to rest wounded limbs on.

Local contractors John Radcliffe & Sons were responsible for construction of the hospital, along with H. Hollingworth & Sons of Moldgreen, joiners, and two men with local connections were appointed to head the medical staff – Dr Marshall, commandant, who was born in Devon but had lived in Huddersfield over thirty years, and Dr Coward, registrar, who was born in South Africa but had lived in Huddersfield for twenty years.

The wards were built with the south-facing wall made of canvas blinds rather that solid wall. This allowed the blinds to be raised during warm weather so the soldiers could benefit from the fresh air. Accommodation was provided for 500 soldiers, but over the course of the war extra associated wards, such as that at the United Methodist schoolrooms, were opened in the area to accommodate even more.

The hospital had one of the lowest death rates in the country and seems to be have been well-liked by the soldiers treated there. One autograph book, which still survives (now in the possession of Royds Hall School), was given to nurse Elsie Cook in 1916.

It is full of sketches drawn by the patients, comments, poems. Captain H. A. Soley of the RFA wrote: 'I have been in five or six hospitals and I can say that the best one of the lot is the War Hospital Huddersfield.' Corporal Stanley Dean was equally complimentary when he wrote that 'this hospital and the town remind me of those two old songs "There are kind hearts everywhere" and "Everybody's loved by someone"'.

One soldier even wrote to the *Huddersfield Examiner* to express his thanks. He was another man who had been in other hospitals that were not as good as Huddersfield. In one day, he said, he'd received oranges, apples, chocolates,

Gordon Donaldson in hospital

grapes and cigarettes. Gifts such as these were distributed two or three times a week and every week around 100 of the wounded were taken out to the pictures then to a 'good tea' at the local Conservative Club. 'I hope,' he wrote, 'if any of the people of this town have sons, husbands or brothers in hospital, that they are as well looked after as I have been since I came here.' (HE, 18 February 1916)

That same year the Freemasons of Huddersfield presented the hospital with a fully equipped gym for the recuperating soldiers (HE, 2 June 1916). The following year, F. W. Sykes of Green Lea, Lindley, part of the family who owned the English Card Clothing and were renowned for their philanthropy, gave a further £1,000 for a new ward. Mr Sykes was also responsible for the motorcycle ambulance that was presented to the war hospital in 1917. The sidecar had been adapted to take a single stretcher, which could be loaded from the rear. A joint project by Campion Cycle Co of Nottinghamshire and Hawkes & Sons, coach

Denby Dale Auxiliary staff and patients

builders of Huddersfield, the sidecar had special springs, which made it extremely comfortable for the patient. During the day the patient could see out of the windows, but it was fitted with electric light for use at night. The orderly travelling with the wounded sat behind the motor cycle driver, and could check on the patient by means of a sliding window. It was specially designed for use when only one soldier needed transporting, thus saving the petrol that would have been consumed had the large ambulance car been used.

Private Gordon Donaldson of Spring Street, Greenhead, was sent back 'to

Blighty' and ended up in a hospital, believed to be in Leeds, where he helped form a jazz band with other patients. The photograph on page 49 illustrates some of the means used to move patients around. Gordon is in the wicker bed on wheels and there is a three-wheeled scooter/chair, which even has its own lamp. Behind Gordon are his girlfriend, Edith Oldfield, and her parents, Albert and Fanny. Visitors, patients and nurses often seem to have got together to perform small concerts and entertainments for the wards.

Auxiliary hospitals

The need for hospitals was growing, so it was with great pride that the Holmfirth Auxiliary Hospital was opened by the district surgeon, Sir Berkeley Moynihan, inspector of hospitals in the Northern Command. This hospital provided fourteen beds, though there had already been some provision in Holmfirth from the very beginning of the war. The matron of the hospital, Mrs Frances Roberts, was later awarded the Red Cross medal for her services.

Denby Dale Auxiliary hospital was the result of a request from the Huddersfield war hospital when a convalescent hospital was required. A local committee was set up, which eventually decided that the Victoria Memorial Hall would be an ideal place. With the addition of a bath, better heating and a thorough cleaning, fifty beds were provided for the soldiers. The village had quickly raised the necessary funds to fully equip the wards, interviewed and employed a matron, Miss M. A. Meadows, supported by Sister B. Mainprize and two cooks. Everything else was done by volunteers. The first patients arrived on 12 December 1916. The hospital closed on 28 February 1919.

The Kirkburton military hospital was housed in the drill hall and had room for twenty beds. Miss Inglis, a Red Cross nurse, was the matron assisted by her sister who was a fully qualified nurse. A committee of local ladies formed a rota to undertake all the housekeeping, including cooking. As with all of the auxiliary hospitals, many concerts and entertainments were arranged and wounded soldiers received cheaper prices at the local cinema. One concert was put on specifically to raise funds to buy a gramophone in order to entertain the patients. The concert included songs by Mrs Haidée Maria Outram, wife of the vicar (HC, 19 February 1916). Mrs Outram became the commandant of the Kirkburton hospital and was later awarded an MBE for the work she had done during the war.

In November, Honley opened its auxiliary hospital with room for twenty-four beds, bringing the area to a total of 1,060. Sister Phoebe Coldwell from this hospital was later given a Red Cross award.

Bradley Sanatorium, intended as a TB (tuberculosis) hospital, was instead opened as an auxiliary hospital in 1917 to take wounded soldiers. Even the drill hall was eventually taken over in 1917 as an auxiliary hospital.

As late as July 1918 the Lepton, Kirkheaton and Whitley Upper auxiliary hospital was opened. Provided by the people in the villages, the plan was to use it as a cottage hospital and headquarters of the local St John's Ambulance Brigade after the war.

Red Cross honours for nurses

One bright spot during the war years was the number of Huddersfield nurses who had been awarded honours for their care and devotion to wounded soldiers. Emily Barry, who had been matron at the Royal Infirmary for the previous thirteen years, gained the Red Cross first-class honour, while Sister Alice Bowdler and Nurses E. Fisher and Daisy Hirst all received the second-class honours. These were awarded by the king at Buckingham Palace, so the four ladies had an enjoyable trip down to London too.

Further awards were made at various times to nurses N. Allen, M. E. Booth, E. Ramsey, Sisters Dorothy Riggall, J. Hawson, Gertrude Butler and Gertie Inman, and Staff Nurse M. Cook. Notice of all awards appeared in the *London Gazette* and *The Times*.

Charities and fundraising

Even though it was agreed that the war would be 'over by Christmas', a great effort would obviously be needed to help the families left behind to deal with wounded soldiers and provide many of the extras needed by the fighting soldiers. Meetings were held in the Town Hall to start this off and offices were afterwards opened on Ramsden Street for women to go along and volunteer their services. Requests included: sewing, knitting, visiting, interpreters, office work, messengers, houses for convalescents, nurses, gifts of all kinds such as money,

Town Hall, Huddersfield

red flannel for bed jackets, twill for shirts, pillow-cases, towels, and wool for socks. Everyone was expected to 'do their bit', no matter how small a contribution they felt they could make. Funds were also needed to buy materials that could be handed out to women to make into whatever was required. The deputy mayoress, Doris Scott Thomson, headed this particular appeal but many women formed their own little groups and held knitting sessions to produce socks or coffee mornings to raise funds.

These organisational skills seem to have been a product of the many groups and societies that women and girls already belonged to – YWCA, Girl Guides, Mother's Union, Queen Mary's Needlework Guild – as well as the Women's Suffrage movement.

War relief fund

The Prince of Wales had set up a fund to help the families of soldiers away fighting. Although initially a national fund, each area administered the funds locally. Separation allowances were paid directly to the soldiers' wives, but the Poor Law Guardians had already needed to pay out small sums to relieve the immediate distress caused by the breadwinner having to leave his job as well as his family.

Local churches set up their own funds too. The Mount Pleasant Methodist Church Leaders' minutes note that 'the collection taken on Sunday 16 August in aid of a Distress Fund for needy cases in connection with our church and school during war amounted to three pound, twelve shillings and nine pence (£3.76)'. They continued to raise funds throughout the war to send parcels to soldiers who were members of their congregation, as well as helping their families. (NH/HSC/8)

Women and their Bit was the heading to an article in the *Huddersfield Examiner* on 24 July 1916. It described the work done by the Huddersfield & District Women's Committee, started by Mrs Kilner Clarke for the wounded soldiers and later taken over by Mrs Blamires and others.

At the outbreak of war, thousands of war charities had been set up, regulated in September 1915 by the Director General of Voluntary Organisations. All the districts around Huddersfield were linked in, via the central depot on Ramsden Street. Links were also made to war hospitals, local army corps and up to the central London organisation.

In the receiving room, goods such as cloth, flannel, wool for knitting, cigarettes, stationery, and so on, were sorted and stored. Items could then be requisitioned and sent direct to wherever they were needed. Women around the borough and district were involved in producing socks (knitted to specified standards), small muslin bags filled with sphagnum moss to be used as dressings at the hospital, mosquito nets, puggarees (cloth bands that were wound around

Advertisement for suitable presents

the helmet to protect against sword cuts – different regiments folded it differently), and even anti-vermin pants and vests, which were made with specially produced material soaked in carbolic acid. That these were badly needed (if not very effective) is shown by this verse:

> Night and day you get no rest,
> Troubled with this dreadful pest
> And they never will be beaten
> While there's any flesh uneaten
> And they'll give no peace until
> Kaiser Bill has paid the bill.

by WHW (extract from a long poem on the subject written in the Royds Hall autograph book).

Some of the items were collected, or made at home but sewing machines were donated for use in the Ramsden Street rooms too. At the time of the newspaper report, 34,000 socks had already been sent, with a further 10,000 in the pipeline.

Households not only sent items to their own men but contributed to other organisations, such as churches, which sent gifts or 'comforts' as they were known to men who had belonged to their particular society. One retailer, Rushworth's, were keen to ensure that the gifts were acceptable, lightweight and bought from them. They advertised regularly in the *Huddersfield Examiner* to offer guidance on which toiletries, writing materials and other practical items were available.

The issuing of a second year report coincided 'with a new phase of the war, in which the fighting is of such a desperate character that no words are wanted to emphasise the great and continuing need of every effort that we can make' (HE, 24 July 1916).

Often the women involved in charity work came from well-off homes, where they had never been expected to work for themselves. They took the opportunity of getting out of the house, rolled up their sleeves and undertook every task from collecting money, making items, visiting the sick or families of soldiers and working as orderlies in the auxiliary hospitals.

Other collection days supported myriad needs, including one to support France, when tricolour flags were made and sold. The frequent comments regarding Huddersfield's lack of recruitment stung the editor of the *Huddersfield Examiner* to comment on 12 July 1915:

> 'Whatever may be said against the people of Huddersfield after the war is over one thing is certain and that is that our Allies will always remember the generous response that was made to the various appeals on their behalf during the most eventful period of the conflict.'

Those at sea were not forgotten either. In July 1916 a major Sailor's Day event was held. In St George's Square a large tank was erected in which a diver showed the sort of work he would undertake beneath the waves, parts of the wreckage of the *John Fielden* lifeboat. In October 1914, the hospital ship HMHS *Rohilla* hit the rocks near Whitby. The *John Fielden* had been one of the six lifeboats to try to rescue the people on board. A new lifeboat, named *'Mary Blamires'* after the mayoress, was also on show. Over 120,000 flags were sold to the spectators, who were encouraged to attend dressed up as characters from the various films on show in the town that week. The whole procession, accompanied by various bands and the pink elephant from the Huddersfield opera, then processed to Greenhead Park where all were able to watch a variety of circus-type acts such as Punch and Judy, Japanese gymnasts the Tykoo Trio, and ventriloquists. Sports for wounded soldiers were also demonstrated. The proceeds of this day were shared between the Royal National Lifeboat Institution, the Seaman's Misson and the Minesweepers.

Although fraud seems to have been rare, it was decided that, with so many people involved in raising money for all sorts of purposes, more control was needed. The War Charities Act was passed in 1916, forcing all war charities to register and anyone collecting on their behalf must be officially approved by that charity. This included any sales, entertainments or exhibitions. Activities by children were also affected. No longer could small groups of children knock on doors asking for funds or make little gifts to sell unless under the auspices of a specified charity.

The local council had to ensure that all organisations were run properly with accounts, a committee of not less than three people, and formal minutes of meetings. Monies raised had to be paid into a separate bank account.

The Poor Law

This covered such social aspects as housing, health, support for the poor and elderly, although there were many welfare reforms at the beginning of the twentieth century, such as old age pensions (1908) and national insurance for unemployment (1911). In 1916 the meeting of Poor Law officers for the whole region was held in Huddersfield. Emily Siddon, the chairman of the Huddersfield Board of Guardians, was there to welcome them, saying it was good for them all to work together. The vice-chairman, E. Whitwam, talked about the changes and improvements over the past thirty years but added that they 'were obliged to anticipate that the future would have more serious problems to be solved …' (HE, 21 February 1916)

In October of the same year, a meeting of Poor Law nurses was held in Huddersfield. Once again Emily Siddon was there to welcome them to the town and speak in support of their efforts in providing nursing care in the workhouses, despite the demands made on their profession by the war. (*The British Journal of Nursing*, 14 October 1916)

Miss Siddon was also president of the Huddersfield branch of the National Union of Women's Suffrage Societies and played a very important role in the life of Huddersfield's Suffrage activities, as well as working tirelessly for the Board of Guardians. A.C. Brook refers to her as 'probably regarded as Huddersfield's most formidable woman in public life'. (Brook, A. C., unpublished PhD thesis) After the war she was awarded an MBE for her services. When she died in 1923 she had been a member of the Board of Guardians for over forty years.

Prisoners-of-war

As far back as the seventeenth century, agreement had been reached about the release of prisoners-of-war after hostilities ceased, and the Hague Convention of 1907 dealt with the treatment of prisoners-of-war. Most European countries agreed to abide by this, although not always as strictly as perhaps they should. Food was the main problem, but then all countries had shortages of food. What was available was used, first of all, for the troops before civilians, and prisoners-of-war were considered. British prisoners-of-war were, therefore, in need of the parcels sent by their families and the Red Cross.

Switzerland provided an invaluable resource in that they took in some prisoners who needed medical treatment and provided them with care, though they were not allowed home until after the war. One lucky prisoner was Private Harry Day, who had been caretaker at the Yorkshire Bank in the Market Place before the war. He had been taken prisoner in August 1914, but because of the harsh treatment and poor diet whilst in a prisoner-of-war camp in Germany, he had become ill. He was transferred to Switzerland, where he was housed in a hotel and 'making a good recovery, thanks to good treatment and food' (HE, 9 November 1916). His wife was even able to go and visit him, courtesy of the Red Cross.

National Motor Volunteers

This organisation had been set up by private motorists in 1915 under the aegis of the National Volunteer Training Corps with a view to providing transport as needed for war work, particularly transporting injured soldiers from the railway station out to the various hospitals. As well as motoring duties, they attended drill lessons and had training in ambulance work.

As part of these duties, and as a recruitment drive, the volunteers held a full car parade in 1916 in order to take wounded soldiers from the war hospital out to Langsett for a breath of fresh air. They appealed for all 'patriotic car owners'

Railway Station, Huddersfield

to join up (HE, 21 July 1916).

By early 1917 they had organised a rota to meet trains arriving after trams and other direct trains had ceased running, and taking 'weary soldiers who live at a distance' (HE, 2 February 1917) to their homes. The cars waited from 10 pm on Sunday and from 10.30 pm on other nights until 2 am when the mail train reached Huddersfield. There were always eight men on duty, who ensured a supply of hot coffee, soup and sandwiches were available and kept the rest room clean and tidy – as well as washing up and drying the pots.

Most nights there were between fourteen and thirty soldiers to be ferried around not just Huddersfield but out as far as Batley, Wakefield, Bradford, Denholme, Skelmanthorpe and Denby Dale. Often they were not just Huddersfield men but French and Belgian soldiers too. One soldier arrived asking to go to Slades, but having no idea where it was. Apparently his wife had written to him to let him know that she had 'flitted' and to give him the new address. Fortunately one of the drivers on duty that night was from the Colne Valley and could take the soldier straight home.

There were also groups of soldiers who arrived at the station after all the trains had gone but needed to wait until a connection arrived the next day before they could continue their journey home. Fortunately, Lloyds Bank had a building in St George's Square, which they intended to open after the war. So in the meantime they allowed the Motor Volunteer Reserve to use the building as a rest room, not just for soldiers during the day but for those who needed just a few hours sleep before continuing their journey. The rest room was officially opened on Saturday 10 February but in fact was used by seven soldiers on the Friday night while the MVR also took home a further twenty-two soldiers. At the opening ceremony fifty wounded soldiers were provided with transport so they could be brought in to enjoy tea and entertainment.

Later that same year a claim was made by Birmingham that it was the first town to begin this kind of transport for the soldiers, a claim that was quickly refuted in the local newspaper (HE, 6 September 1917). Here it was pointed out that Huddersfield not only provided transport but a rest room and operated on Sundays too. In the previous week over 1,000 wounded soldiers had used the rest room, twenty-one had stayed overnight and more than 200 had been met at the station and taken home – the drivers completing a total of nearly 800 miles between them. All of this was done on a voluntary basis, with petrol provided by the motorists themselves.

In 1918 the name was changed to the West Riding Army Service Corps Motor Transport.

A concert party in France

Although it is often thought that the reality of the war was not known in Britain, this is not really the case. Not only did soldiers write home, often making quite open comments about the mud, the rain and cold, and the bombing, but some people went to France and returned with vivid reports.

Lena Ashwell was a Northumbrian actress who had asked the government if she could take concert parties out to entertain the troops. Though refused official permission she nevertheless sent out small groups of artistes anyway, under the auspices of the women's auxiliary of the YWCA. In October 1916 she had arrived in Huddersfield to talk to the local Women's Committee for Soldiers and Sailors about her work, detailing the 'horror … the intense despair of it all … to see fine men going up to the line and battered wrecks coming down' (HE, 25 October 1916). Her plea for continued support to keep up the morale of the soldiers did not go unheard.

In February 1917, a musical group from Huddersfield, including Lottie Beaumont (contralto), Constance Wilkinson (soprano), Elsie Beanland (violinist) and Haydn Sandwell (accompanist, and also organist at St Stephen's Church, Lindley), arrived in France, to find themselves greeted by a young man from Lindley – Wesley Wilman. They were then taken by car to their hotel, where they immediately gave an impromptu concert to the officers there, afterwards being told they were 'one of the more talented parties to have crossed the water' (HE, 7 March 1917). They worked hard, giving two or three concerts each day in makeshift theatres, sometimes with long journeys between. At one camp, the room was so packed the men were hanging on the roof railings and sitting on the roof crossbeams. Backdrops were old army blankets and lighting was provided by oil lamps. Concerts were given in hospitals, garages, airplane hangars; to soldiers about to go to the Front, or just returned; to those wounded and to those looking after them; to British, Australian and Canadian troops. They even managed to visit the army veterinary camp to see how horses were cared for. The singers suffered from the cold and wind, getting sore throats from having to sing over the roar of the guns, but managed to provide twenty-seven concerts in fourteen days, entertaining 25,000 people.

YMCA

This organisation, begun in the early nineteenth century to provide leisure activities for lads who might otherwise be involved in excessive drinking and criminal activity, also provided huts for the soldiers at the Front or in training camps. There they could relax, have some refreshment, read papers, listen to lectures on a variety of subjects or watch concerts. The *Huddersfield Examiner* (15 February 1916) printed a report from J. W. Scholefield, the secretary of the Huddersfield YMCA, because the town had financed two huts in France. Though these were nominally for Huddersfield men, movement of the troops meant that no hut was used exclusively by any particular group but was a welcome relief to all. Mr Schofield was taking charge of the larger of the two huts, whilst Reverend W. Hastwell, the congregationalist minister from Moldgreen, looked after the other.

> 'Efforts are being made to get photographs taken, but the military regulations on this question are exceedingly strict,' they said. 'Men come in from the trenches weary and tired at all hours of the day and night and whatever time it is hot coffee, cakes, chocolates and cigarettes are available for them at practically cost price … sometimes they fall asleep on the floor and only wake up in time to go back to their duty in the firing line.'

They were expecting a visit from the commander-in-chief, Sir Douglas Haig, and Schofield explained

> 'we are arranging to place large boards outside each hut with the words "Huddersfield Hut" painted on them so that every soldier using them will know to whom his thanks are due for these specific huts.'

YMCA huts at home included one in the grounds of British Dyes Ltd, one in auxiliary hospitals at Bradley Gate and Royds Hall, as well as a YWCA in town for the influx of women coming to work in the factories and mills. In 1917 there was a further appeal to raise funds for another YMCA hut near the drill hall. In explaining the work of the organisation it was commented that;

> 'a grateful country would do everything for a man as long as he was able to shoulder a rifle, but the danger was that it would forget him when he was no longer able to take his place in the firing line.' The YMCA tried to plug the gap with sanitoria for those with consumption (tuberculosis) and

employment agencies for those seeking work, as well as providing the amenities of the huts themselves (HE, 9 October 1917). The money needed was raised within a few weeks. The eventual aim of the association was to set up a Red Triangle Club in each village around Huddersfield so that when the soldiers came home, they could continue their membership.

Souvenirs

Many soldiers brought their own souvenirs home from the war. In January 1917, Colonel Louis Demetriadi, a doctor from Huddersfield, returned home on leave and gave a talk on the value of the presents, food parcels and so on sent by Huddersfield people to the army on the continent. He also brought many artefacts home with him, such as a British rifle smashed by a German machine-gun, a helmet originally belonging to a doctor in the Prussian Army and a very ordinary tin helmet from a British soldier, which still had the dents made by the shrapnel. This ordinary helmet had saved a man's life. German gas masks and a bayonet were on show as well as a bomb, shells, fuses, cartridges and bullets. These were all displayed in the Town Hall and many went to view them. A suggestion was also made for a local war museum, to show exhibits from various wars with details of the local battalions.

Though there was some enthusiasm for this, it never actually came to fruition. Many years later, the Bullecourt Museum was opened privately in the drill hall

Great War Exhibits, Bullecourt Museum

in Milnsbridge, where similar artefacts (and many more) can still be seen.

Demetriadi had been in the Territorial Force so had been called up on the day war was declared, accompanying the 1/5th battalion of the Dukes as their medical officer. By April 1915 he had been appointed colonel in charge of the West Riding Clearing Hospital in France and had twice been mentioned in despatches, once by Lord French and once by General Sir Douglas Haig. Unfortunately, ill health prevented him from returning to active service. In October 1918 he died and was

Drill Hall, Milnsbridge

later buried with full military honours in St Stephen's Church, Lindley, where he had been churchwarden for four years.

Animals in the War

Soldiers were not the only ones needed at the Front. Although lorries, armoured cars, tanks and other vehicles were in use or being developed, thousands of horses were needed for transport and the cavalry was still considered important in the field of battle. Despite the need for horses for farm work, many were requisitioned and had to be given up to the Army. The local Military Training Corps appealed too for the loan of horses for the Mounted Battalion.

One horse from Huddersfield got a tearful send off. Ivy Tucker Clayton lived

War Horse poster from the Blue Cross

with her grandparents, who were farmers, at Syke Field on New Hey Road. On 26 August 1914, the *Huddersfield Examiner* stated that: 'There had been a farewell ceremony, and when the little mare was marched off she carried with her the tokens of a child's sorrow. Tied to the horse with a piece of blue ribbon were a label and a sprig of heather, and on the label was written this message: "Sorry she has to leave us. Hope she will return to us safe and sound. With much love." And beneath the words were crosses that were eloquent in their profusion.'

Later the newspaper was able to report that a gunner from the Royal Horse Artillery had taken the trouble to write back to reassure the little girl that the horse had arrived safely and would be carefully looked after. Though the soldier hoped she would soon recover her pet, it was most unlikely. Millions of horses died in appalling circumstances during the course of the war and, even if they did survive, few were brought back to England.

Almost as soon as war was declared, the RSPCA began a fund to provide ambulances, hospitals and veterinary treatment, as well as shelters, head collars and bandages for horses at the Front. The Duke of Portland became its chairman and so the fund was known as the Duke of Portland's Fund for Sick and Wounded Horses. The *Huddersfield Examiner* frequently carried appeals for this fund.

Our Dumb Friends League (ODFL) had earlier started their Blue Cross fund to help animals during the Balkan War of 1912, so were able to continue this and provide a similar service to the many animals that were used between 1914 and 1918. At the Annual General Meeting of the RSPCA in 1915 the Huddersfield branch donated £5 towards the Blue Cross in support of its work as both charities helped to provide much needed assistance to the war animals.

War Horse Day

Early on in the war, Driver James McKenzie of Holmfirth wrote to a friend about the difficulty of life at the Front, not just for the men but for the animals. 'We see some sorry reminders here in the shape of horses who are suffering from the rigour and hardships of war.' (HE, 6 June 1915) As it became obvious that more money was needed, it was decided to hold a War Horse Day to collect money for the animal hospitals set up by the RSPCA and the Blue Cross. The initial requests for help included reference to the role of horses in the Boer War, which had ended only twelve years previously, and the monument, 'the only one in the world erected to the memory of horses which have fallen in war' (HE, 15 July 1915), built in Port Elizabeth, South Africa.

It was decided to have horse shoe badges and emblems for the day, with a procession to leave St George's Square. *The Huddersfield Examiner* invited groups that had a link to horses such as vets, shoe smiths, corn dealers, teamsters, etc, to take part, and asked horse owners to bring their horses. A large number of people lent their time to this event: Miss Watkinson of Rawthorpe Hall, Dalton,

Horse Memorial, Port Elizabeth

who was very heavily involved with the animal charities, Mr J. Brooke of Bradley Mills, H. Garside of the Palace Theatre, S. Winks of the Hippodrome, Mrs A. B. Mountain, J. Rollin Hargreaves and, of course, Inspector Browne of the Huddersfield RSPCA.

On 24 July, thousands of people came – local people who could walk to town, and others who came by tram or train from the surrounding areas – to take part or just to view the procession, which included a zebra brought from the Halifax Zoo by its keeper, S. Hinds. The procession was led by Mr Winks in a motor car, followed by the mayoress in a horse-drawn carriage. After the massive parade had marched around the town, a mock auction was held. One dog, 'bought' by a tripe dresser called Guy Gotherd, was then given back and auctioned again. After the fourth auction, the dog had raised £5 7s (£5.35). Mr Gotherd then donated a Pomeranian, which was 'sold' for 15/- (75p). When all the money had been collected over £1,000 had been raised.

On 4 September 1915, the *Huddersfield Chronicle* published a letter from Arthur J. Coke, who was the secretary of ODFL. He had been in France inspecting the Blue Cross hospitals there. In Moret there were four hospitals, made up of fourteen wards for 200 horses. Provins also had four hospitals containing almost as many horses in seven wards, whilst Troyes had three hospitals for 125 horses. He described how one horse had been taken in with nineteen shrapnel wounds that had had to be extracted over two painful days. One bullet, in fact, had only just missed the vital areas of the neck. Not surprisingly, there was also a plea for funds to continue with this important work. The hospital in Moret named 'Huddersfield' specialised in surgery and pharmacy work, where horses that were contaminated (i.e. had infectious diseases such as mange) could be treated (The Blue Cross at War).

Chapter Four

Employment

In the early part of 1914 trade had been falling. Some mills had gone onto short time or even laid workers off. Flora Lockwood, wife of Josiah Lockwood of Black Rock Mills in Linthwaite, wrote extensive diaries during the war years and comments that at the beginning of August the mill was working only four days a week. This soon changed as the mills secured orders for cloth for uniforms, not just for the British Army but from Russia, Belgium and France too. At the beginning of 1915, 200 miles of cloth were ordered from Lockwood's for French blue-grey worth £120,000. Not surprisingly, Westminster soon brought in a special tax for 'excessive profits' on businesses.

Even *The Times* newspaper was writing articles for the rest of the country about the 'Valley of Khaki' (28 January 1915) where, they suggested, the workforce was 'burning the candle at both ends to keep the troops supplied with khaki'. The Factory Act regulations were relaxed so that women and children could work longer hours too. Workers from the cotton mills of Lancashire were brought in as well as employment being taken up by some of the Belgian refugees. Production, it was said, 'was no longer measured by the yard but by the mile'. The newspaper also suggested that this was one reason why recruitment was lower in the area than elsewhere – the men were too busy working in the mills, in itself a contribution to the war effort.

This contribution was recognised, in 1918, by a visit from King George V and Queen Mary to Huddersfield and some of the textile mills in the area, as well as the new British Dyes company.

Textile trade

As might be expected, the textile trade benefited enormously, in many ways, from the war. The worsted trade was uncertain as most was exported, often to Europe, which posed the problem of possible unemployment in that section of the textile trade, but the woollen trade had many orders from the Allies. Woollen output for the first six months of the year eventually exceeded that of any previous year. Although there was full employment, as men left to join up, trained labour became scarce. Even women were working twelve or thirteen hours a day and youngsters from 14 to 16 were permitted to work nine hours a week too.

However, war shortages had their effect as labour, raw materials and dyes were all in short supply. The workers quickly realised that there was an urgent need for redoubled efforts to meet the needs of the army and promptly went on strike for higher wages. Throughout the war, as the cost of living increased, workers in most of the large industries constantly demanded extra pay and war bonuses.

The English Card Clothing Company, in Lindley, offered their employees a bonus of 2/- (10p) for men over 21 and 1/- (5p) for men under 21 and for women – for the duration of the war only. In May 1916 the General Union of Textile Workers refused to go to arbitration over a demand for a war bonus of 25 per cent plus a quarter penny per hour extra for all male workers. Fettlers, who had been on unofficial strike for a week, received summonses because their work came under the Munitions Act, which made strikes illegal.

Most of the strikes were for higher wages to keep pace with the rise in prices. Prior to the war butter had cost 10d (4p) per pound but had risen to 1/2d (6p). Two pounds of sugar had risen from 4d (1½p) to 1/- (5p) while meat had doubled in price from 8d (3p) a pound to 1/6d (7p).

Not all absentees were on strike. In July 1916 almost 300 munitions workers were summoned for being absent from work over the Whitsuntide holidays in June. Factories affected included David Brown & Sons Ltd, William Whiteley & Sons Ltd, Thomas Broadbent & Sons Ltd, W. C. Holmes & Co Ltd and Calvert & Co Ltd. There was a 'boisterous procession to the Town Hall to appear before

English Card Clothing, Acre Mill

the General Munitions Tribunal' (HE, 5 July 1916).

It had been agreed that the Whitsuntide holidays would be postponed until after July as the country needed more supplies. The move had been agreed with the unions but the meeting in Huddersfield had been late, and the men had demanded time-and-a-half for Whitsuntide Monday instead of the nationally agreed time-and-a-quarter. Most workers continued to work as agreed but the above firms suffered substantial problems because of the absentees.

The verdict of the tribunal was that the men had acted out of thoughtlessness, but 'they must realise that, though they were tired from work, these were difficult times and must put their own feelings aside and support the lads putting their lives in danger to secure our liberties' (HE, 5 July 1916). The fines, which could have been up to £3 per day, ranged from 1/- (5p) up to 25/- (£1.25), depending on earnings.

Both employers and tribunals had to deal with the problem of conscientious objectors. The Education Committee had previously agreed that any teachers who were transferred or imprisoned as a result of their beliefs would be reinstated after the war. At a meeting in October, Alderman Beaumont wanted to have this agreement rescinded, making the comments that they 'could not be trusted with children … who needed to learn about responsibility to the state, to be brave, honourable and willing to lay down their lives, to love freedom, liberty and truth … [to learn to detest] cowards and shirkers' (HE, 13 October 1916). Councillor Topping considered these 'nasty, vindictive remarks', but the vote on the matter was lost by only four votes. A further motion, simply to 'consider' applications by teachers who were conscientious objectors, was carried.

This was not the only controversial view at that meeting. Alderman Smith wanted to reduce the war bonus paid to women teachers from 2/- (10p) to 1/- (5p), as women didn't feel the pinch the same as men – despite the fact that most were, by this time, the breadwinners of the households. Smith wanted to give the extra money to the male teachers instead. Fortunately, this was not the view of the rest of the committee.

Full employment brought considerable prosperity to Huddersfield and its industries. E. Brook Ltd (later becoming Brook Motors and eventually Brook Crompton), manufacturers of motors and gears, had been founded in 1904 with works in Threadneedle Street before moving to Nelson Mill on Colne Road. In 1917, continuous expansion necessitated a further move into purpose-built works at St Thomas Road, Longroyd Bridge. The modern building had space for over 200 employees and included a subsidised canteen, where the workers were treated to high tea and a whist drive and dance.

Other businesses were not so lucky. In February 1915, a massive fire completely destroyed the Crosland Moor Mills belonging to G. Crosland & Sons Ltd. The mill had been running night and day, working on government orders for khaki and grey cloth for the Russian army.

Map of Paddock showing Crosland Moor Mills

The fire began in some condensing machinery and within fifteen minutes the whole mill was ablaze. The workforce was quickly evacuated. Those at the Oldfield Street end were able to use a new fire escape, but those nearest to

Manchester Road had to smash the windows to get out. Two boys became trapped in the weaving shed, which was already aflame, but were eventually rescued through the roof. The fire brigade could do nothing to stop the fire but managed to keep it from spreading, while some of the workforce rescued a large amount of stock and raw materials. As the building began to collapse, each floor dropping on to the one below, some of the debris fell through telephone wires and cut off communication through the Manchester-Leeds junction. Trams stopped running and traffic had to be diverted away from the area. Over 500 people were thrown out of work, though it was felt that, because of the amount of work in other mills, they would soon find new jobs. The damage was so extensive that the mill was not rebuilt.

In 1917, for the first time in months, the textile industry had to go on short time in order to conserve supplies of wool and cotton. Weekend work was curtailed and mills often closed on Friday afternoon, reducing hours from fifty-five to forty-five, with consequent loss of pay for their workers.

The Munitions Court heard many cases of men wishing to move jobs and demanding a leaving certificate from their employers. Women often wanted to change jobs too. Mary Hannah Smith was employed at Longwood Gas Company as a gas meter inspector. She complained to the court that they had withheld her insurance card as well as a leaving certificate. She described her work as collecting the money when emptying the meters – often up to £16 in coppers, which could weigh around 80lb. Her employers did not even give her a bag to carry the money in and expected her to carry heavy equipment with which to test the meters. The court decided she was being treated unfairly and ordered the certificates to be handed over as soon as possible.

British dyewares

Since war began the question of how to ensure there were sufficient dyes for the textile industry had been discussed. The German chemical industry was the most advanced in the world and the majority of British textile firms bought dyes from there.

The discussion eventually led to the formation of the British Dyes Company Ltd. After much deliberation and visits to other sites around the country, it was announced in October that the factory would be built in Huddersfield with a directorship made up of men primarily from the Huddersfield area. Huddersfield's advantages included a good labour supply, good communications, particularly by rail, with nearby canal facilities, which could easily take 100-ton barges, and plentiful supplies of coal, electricity and water. In total, 450 acres of land were purchased for the industry – 250 for the actual buildings and 200 as a buffer zone, though it was stated in the newspaper that only colours would be produced, not explosives.

Picric acid, known as Lyddite, had been produced in Huddersfield during the Boer War and by December 1915 even more was being produced. In 1916 the Munitions (Liability for Explosions) Act had to be passed whereby the government accepted liability for damages caused by explosions at such factories (WYK/1075). By 1917, more land had been purchased in Bradley and a plant built to produce picric acid from phenol. Despite this, very little appeared in the *Huddersfield Examiner* relating to anything other than the production of dyes.

There was, initially, a very positive attitude to the establishment of the industry in Huddersfield, with the expectation of an expansion of the town to accommodate the expected influx of labourers and their families. Perhaps the inhabitants of Huddersfield might not have been so happy about the placing of the factory had they realised its implications.

Health and Safety, though not as stringent as today's working world, was still enforced during war years. The rapid building of dyeworks and munitions factories around the Leeds Road area put a strain on facilities, including sewerage works. Some of the workers began to suffer 'chemical eczema', which was partly caused by insanitary conditions but also because the workers tended to use whichever gloves were handy, thus spreading any disease. The company issued gloves to each employee personally and forbade them to use anyone else's gloves while at work. This finally brought the dermatitis under control.

Less easy to control were fatalities. Edith Staley, who was only 27 years old, lived in Golcar with her husband Edward. They both worked for the same chemical manufacturer. Edith worked in the TNT department initially, where she had to work down a pit, but this made her feel sick. After a four-week absence due to sickness, she was moved into the benzol and toluol department, which did not affect her as much.

On 23 December 1917, a spanner was dropped 'from 30 feet' and hit Edith on the head, causing concussion. She was initially treated at the works but later saw her own doctor, Dr Ratray. He redressed the wound to her head. Another doctor, Dr Baldwin, also saw her at some point and said she had jaundice, but that was the last time this was mentioned. All care was then undertaken by Dr Ratray and his assistant Dr Braithwaite. Neither diagnosed jaundice, despite the fact that she appears to have become worse and turned very yellow. Eventually, she was admitted to the Royal Infirmary where she died. Cause of death was given as toxic jaundice, which had considerably reduced the size of her liver. The inquest verdict was accidental death from TNT poisoning accelerated by the blow on the head (HE, 17 January 1917).

In 1918, the *Huddersfield Examiner* reported on an inquest on the foreman at the chemical works. Abraham Bradley, of Thornton Road had returned home on 28 December 1917 complaining of pains in his inside. Dr Pullan prescribed medicine, but did not actually attend the patient. Bradley died a few days later. Other workmates said Bradley had complained before about feeling ill. Though the fumes in the shed where they worked were not harmful, fumes from other sheds were. When Bradley had seen his own doctor some weeks prior to his death, he had said that a pan had boiled over and he'd breathed in the fumes. The post mortem showed he had been poisoned by picric acid, nitrobenzene or arsenic. The verdict was accidental death and the firm expressed regret at losing a valuable worker.

A new college dept

British Dyes later donated £5,000 towards the building and equipping of a new research department at the technical college. Britain was still lagging behind Germany in chemistry and its uses in industry. Huddersfield Council 'hoped that the manufacturers, dyers and the public spirited men of the town would take it to heart and that in a very short time they would have such a magnificent block of buildings as might eventually be termed "The Huddersfield University"' (HE, 20 July 1916).

Others expressed the wish that after the war Huddersfield would be the centre of the production of colours and dyes for the world, which would lead to the growth of the town in size and prosperity. For this to happen, more investment would be needed. In September 1918, appeals were made to build and furnish new areas for textile, chemical and engineering departments. It was pointed out that any students wanting practical instruction in scribbling and spinning had to go to Leeds University or Batley. Worsted had no practical areas at all, students had to go to Halifax (HE, 25 September 1918).

Women in the war

As men were leaving the town to go to the Front, employers realised that they could no longer function unless they found substitute workers. The tramways, particularly, were hit hard as many of the men they employed had been reservists and were therefore the first to be called up. Over thirty men had rejoined the colours in the first weeks of the war and many other tram employees were in the Territorials and were leaving regularly. It was difficult to train new men quickly enough.

By July the solution appeared in the form of 'four attractive young ladies learning the duties of tram conducting' (HE, 28 July 1915). The ladies were considered very business-like, wearing the crossover belts, with bell punch and cash bag. The tram manager, R. H. Wilkinson, explained that the women were having to be employed to fill the jobs left vacant by those who had already volunteered, made even more difficult by a policy of not employing any man who was fit for military service. He asked the public for their 'kind co-operation', including an appeal to the motormen (tram drivers) to assist the females in carrying out their duties.

The most vexing question appeared to be that of uniform. The sub-committee of the Tramways Committee asked their wives for help, the women themselves were consulted and photographs of uniforms designed by other tram companies around the country were all considered before the final decision was made – navy blue serge with red piping and gilt buttons on the coat, a hat of navy serge and red piping with a red badge on the front with the Corporation monogram. It did, apparently, resemble the usual men's uniform as much as possible.

Most of the public seem to accept the change readily, though some men were rather condescending. One made the unkind comment that the women were only out looking for a husband, to which the tram conductress promptly replied that 'all the decent men had gone to the Front' (HE, 27 Aug 1915).

A few days later the newspaper reported on yet another 'Patriotic Action'. Kathleen Mary Mitchell, an 18-year-old girl, had offered to drive the van belonging to pork butcher Frank Cooper so that his former driver could volunteer to become a transport driver in the army. Since Mary's father was a local motor engineer, Charles Hirst Mitchell, she already had a good knowledge of vehicles and was a competent driver. She later became the only woman in the National Motor Volunteers, who provided transport for the wounded soldiers.

Since around 8000 men had left Huddersfield to join the forces many machines were left idle until women could be trained to take over their jobs. There was an influx of women workers into munitions work of all kinds. They came mainly from North and East Yorkshire and the East Midlands, causing a greater need for accommodation and transport.

The Huddersfield Women's Hostel was regularly packed to capacity with women coming in search of employment and with wives of wounded soldiers who had been sent to the area to be treated, lodgings were at a premium.

The winter of 1917 was one of the worst, both in length and intensity, in England and in Europe. There were huge snowdrifts along the Colne Valley – up to 10 feet deep at Standedge. Ashes were spread by the council but the roads remained very slippery. What was described as a 'hurricane' hit the area in the early hours of 9 January, tearing down three telegraph poles (HE, 10 January 1917).

At the beginning of April, just as everyone thought it was ending, a massive snowstorm and blizzard struck the area. A report in the *Huddersfield Examiner* on 3 April told of the problems postgirls were having in delivering the mail, though all deliveries were completed. 'One confessed to shedding tears at the work load' while another had caused great concern because of her late return. She explained that she'd 'had to go breast-high in snow in places'. But all the girls went out on their second deliveries, despite being given the option not to go.

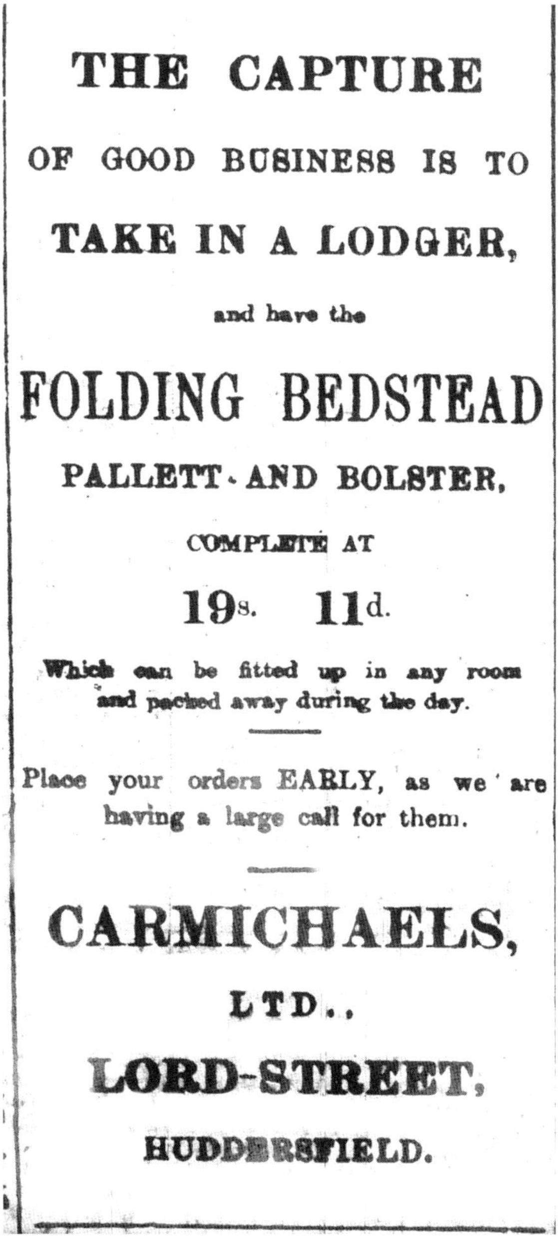

Advertisement for equipping a lodger's room

New Summer Time Act

For the first time, British people had to get used to the concept of moving time. The idea had been introduced eight years earlier but the Daylight Saving Bill was thrown out by the House of Commons. However, Germany adopted the idea in 1916 and, not to be outdone, the Summer Time Act came into force in Britain on Sunday 21 May 1916, and all clocks had to be put forward by one hour in order to give more light in the evenings to save fuel and make better use of available time for work. Police and night workers would, on the changeover day, be working one hour less and were paid accordingly.

In September, posters and notices appeared reminding everyone that 'summertime' had ended and clocks needed to be put back one hour. The notices included instruction on how to do this – either stop the clock for one hour or wind the hour-hand eleven times forwards, with pauses for the striking points. Serious damage could be done to clocks or watches if anyone tried to wind them backwards.

Chapter Five

Recreation

Huddersfield had a wealth of small societies, reflecting such interests as growing flowers and vegetables on the allotments and in gardens. Slaithwaite Flower Show was cancelled initially but by 1915 daily life seemed to be back to normal. The summer of 1915 saw the tenth annual Horticultural Society show at the Mechanics Hall with only a few less entries that previously, as did a similar show at Linthwaite.

Church sales of work were usually held to raise funds for the church, but during the war the funds were often split with various war charities. When Milnsbridge Wesleyan Church held its sale of work in 1915 it was with a definite military feeling as the hall was decorated with Union Jacks and the colours of all the Allies. The sale was usually held at Christmas but 'unlike the soldiers, they were downhearted when war broke out and postponed the event' (HE, 22 February 1915).

Sports clubs abounded – rugby league being founded in Huddersfield as recently as 1895. There were, therefore, considerable differences in reaction as to whether any of these activities were legitimate during the war.

The feeling had been, in autumn 1914, that Germany was on the run so there was no need to cancel any matches. Though this was proved a false hope, football still continued and was reported in great detail, along with cricket matches in the region. It was pointed out in the *Huddersfield Chronicle* in September 1914 that not everyone was able to enlist, but clubs should offer facilities for them to do so if possible. No bonuses should be given to players and any gaps caused by enlistment should be filled with local lads, even if they were not good players. In fact, Huddersfield Rugby Club had one of its most successful seasons during the war years. Sports-mad young men also had the chance to start military training with a rifle range in the large distribution corridor at Leeds Road.

Rowland Hely Owen, son of a local solicitor, had played for Yorkshire but in a letter to his parents, which subsequently appeared in the paper, he pleaded for the sportsmen to join up. He sent a copy of a cartoon showing a wounded soldier with a fallen comrade in Flanders. In the background a crowd is watching a football match at home. The caption reads 'will they never come?' In his letter to the secretary of the rugby club, written from the allied forces hospital in Boulogne, Rowland comments: 'This was going to be our great year. Well, so it will be if we send as many on to the field of battle as we send on to the field of play.' (KX324 letters of R. H. Owen)

Theatres too continued to provide entertainment, often tempering it to the

Hippodrome Cinema

mood of the times. The Hippodrome offered a free showing of *The Pride of Bysantia* to all wives of soldiers or Territorials who had already been called up. Most of the theatres and picture houses allowed the wounded soldiers from the various local hospitals to attend free of charge.

In March 1915, there was even a new cinema. The Empire Picture House, near the railway station, with its stone-coloured neo-Grecian architecture opened with *Kismet*, uplifting if not in the patriotic style.

The Empire later showed the film *The Dummy*, starring Jack Pickford, younger brother of Mary Pickford who was co-founder of the film studio United Artists. The write-up for this film commented that 'in the role of a semi-idiot "the dummy", Jack Pickford has a part well suited to him' (HE, 3 July 1917).

One of the most attended pictures was entitled 'Battle of the Somme' which did, in fact, contain film showing the soldiers going 'over the top', the smoke of bombs, wounded being carried off the field and so on. This was a silent film, accompanied by a pianist who would change the tempo of the music to match the action on screen. Much of the film was taken during the 'great advance' and according to the *Huddersfield Examiner* 'gives some insight into the magnitude of the European struggle'. (HE, 11 September 1916)

Entertainment

As always there was a pantomime over Christmas and New Year. In 1914, the most popular song was *Sister Susie's Sewing Shirts for Soldiers*, as many women were, indeed, busily sewing, not just shirts, but almost every other kind of garment too, to be sent off in parcels to the Front. Honley Palladium scored another hit with *It's a Long Way to Tipperary*. *Cinderella* was on at the Hippodrome while at the Palace so many people turned up that many had to be refused entry.

At the Parochial Hall in Kirkburton the entertainment, in aid of the Soldier's Comfort Fund, was a variety performance with an orchestra playing and a series of sketches. One sketch, called *The Recruit*, was written by Lance-Corporal F. A. Carter from Huddersfield who, according to the vicar, showed 'a fine appreciation of patriotic fervour' (HE, 9 February 1915). The evening raised £9 10s (£9.50). The war certainly did not stop people going out and enjoying themselves.

A common entertainment around Huddersfield was the annual 'Sing', or 'Thump' as it was often called. Most districts had their own version and Longwood Thump is still in existence 100 years later. In 1915, the Holmfirth Sing included many patriotic songs but also hymns such as *Oh God of Love, Oh King of Peace, Make War Throughout the World to Cease* – a hymn from the heart for many. Proceeds over the next years went to various war charities, such as the Holmfirth Military Hospital. (KC201)

But not all forms of recreation were frivolous. The Huddersfield Scouts and Wolf Cubs Association had a variety of exercises including parades, drills, short route marches, band practices, signalling and ambulance classes. For some of the lads, at least, it would be good preparation for their later career in the army.

This year saw the first loss of fireworks on Bonfire Night. No one was allowed to buy their own, but permission for large-scale events could be applied for. No event was allowed after dark in case of bombing or Zeppelin raids, so all had to finish before sunset.

The Pink Elephant

The Original Opera Company (now Huddersfield Light Opera Society), which had already had successful concerts specifically to raise funds during productions in 1914, now decided that, as part of the war effort, they would produce a new opera – *The Pink Elephant*.

Pink Elephant programme cover

The music and score were written by two of their members: Ernest Woodhead and Arthur A. Lodge, with some additional songs by F. V. Lawson and Edred Booth junior.

Mr. E. WOODHEAD, Part Author.

Mr. A. A. LODGE, Part Author and Composer.

E. Woodhead and A. A. Lodge

Rehearsals began in the summer and included a visit to the Moorland Inn at Scammonden, where the group had a picnic as well as their final rehearsal before the summer break. Things did not always run smoothly, however. Lister Brook, who was playing the captain, was not able to perform the full week due to a family bereavement, so his place had to be taken over by the conductor, Charles Bonnett. The first violinist, Harry Field, then had to take over as conductor. The opera was performed at the Theatre Royal from December right through Christmas week, with a full review appearing in the *Huddersfield Chronicle* on 11 January 1916. The part of the king was played by Tom Denham, who was a well-known singer. He was also responsible for designing much of the society's publicity material.

Theatre Royal,

HUDDERSFIELD.

◆ •• ◆

Boxing Day, Monday, Dec. 27th, 1915,

And remainder of Week.

With Matinee, Saturday, Jan. 1st, 1916, at 2-15.

In aid of Local War Relief Funds.

THE HUDDERSFIELD
ORIGINAL OPERA COMPANY,

President : Sir William Raynor, J.P..

In the New and Original Light Opera.

"THE PINK ELEPHANT"

Words by Ernest Woodhead and Arthur A. Lodge.

Music by Arthur A. Lodge
(with added numbers by F. V. Lawton and Edred Booth, Jun.)

Produced under the direction of Mr. Chas. Bonnett
(Late of George Edwardes's and George Dance's Companies).

Musical Director : Mr. Edred Booth, Jun., F.R.C.O., L.R.A.M.

Pink Elephant programme

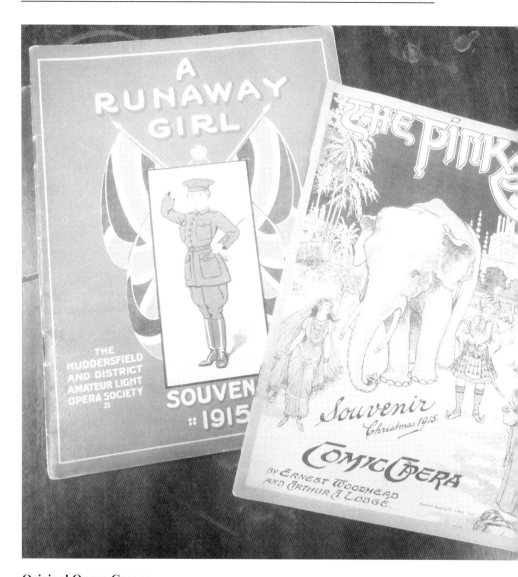

Original Opera Company programmes

On New Year's Day they performed a matinee at which soldiers from the local war hospitals attended. It was a popular way of raising funds: subscribers paid all the costs and profits of over £70 were shared amongst various local war charities. Like many other organisations, the Original Opera Company proudly named all their members who had enlisted.

ROLL OF
HONOUR.

The following Members of the Society are at present serving with His Majesty's Forces, viz:—

Capt. BERNAL SYKES, 7th Battalion Duke of Wellington's West Riding Regt.
Lieut. F. H. THREAPPLETON, 4th Battalion Duke of Wellington's West Riding Regt.
Lieut. W. STANLEY WOOLVEN, 3rd Battalion King's Own Yorkshire Light Infantry.
Second-Lieut. J. HAIGH, 5th Battalion Duke of Wellington's West Riding Regt.
Second Lieut. J. REYNOLDS, 7th Battalion Duke of Wellington's West Riding Regt.
Second-Lieut. J. A. STEPHENS, 9th Battalion East Yorkshire Regt.
Sergt. J. F. ROBERTS, 168th (Huddersfield) Brigade, R.F.A.
Corporal V. CARTWRIGHT, 168th (Huddersfield) Brigade, R.F.A.
Bombardier F. WOOD, 168th (Huddersfield) Brigade, R.F.A.
Driver E. LOCKWOOD, R.F.A.
Corporal GEO. GRANGE, Queen's Own Yorkshire Dragoons.
Corporal L. MITSON, Army Service Corps.
Lance-Corporal J. H. IRONS, 5th Battalion Duke of Wellington's West Riding Regt.
Lance-Corporal W. JONES, 5th Battalion Duke of Wellington's West Riding Regt.
Private P. BENSON, 5th Battalion Duke of Wellington's West Riding Regt.
Private W. BURNHAM, 5th Battalion Duke of Wellington's West Riding Regt.
Private F. CUTTELL, 3rd Battalion Duke of Wellington's West Riding Regt.
Private W. DALE, 5th Battalion Duke of Wellington's West Riding Regt.
Private J. SYKES, 5th Battalion Duke of Wellington's West Riding Regt.
Private L. TOWNEND, 5th Battalion Duke of Wellington's West Riding Regt.
Private J. BROADBENT, Royal Army Medical Corps.
Private C. N. BOOTH, Royal Army Medical Corps.
Private J. E. STREET, Royal Army Medical Corps.

Members of the Society serving in the forces

Chapter Six

Against the law

The Defence of the Realm Act (DORA) was passed in 1914, which allowed the government to act as necessary in defence. It covered many aspects of life and was amended during the course of the war. Some of its provisions included not being able to talk in public places or spread rumours about military matters or anything that might prejudice the war effort. Photographing military establishments was also prevented, as was importing or keeping homing pigeons or having wireless telegraphic equipment without permission. Bonfires, fireworks, ringing church bells were all banned. Pub hours were curtailed and buying drinks for others was disallowed. The government gave itself the powers to take over factories, land or censor the newspapers.

Despite the general air of patriotism and attitudes of helping each other, there were plenty who continued to help themselves instead. James Littlewood, 51, a millhand at a local dyeworks, was convicted of theft from the military stores at Uppermill, stealing eight shirts, two pairs of drawers, two pairs of socks, one woollen body belt, one pair of boots, two leather belts, one razor and one strap, the property of the 7th Battalion, West Riding Regiment. All the property was recovered except two shirts he'd already passed on to his son-in-law. Although Littlewood denied the theft at first, he finally admitted that he'd received them from his eldest son, Wilson, who was in the 7th Battalion.

A further case of a crime created because of the war was that of an English woman who had married a German. Gertrude Zebach was affected by the Aliens' Restriction Orders. She had ensured that she got a permit from the Huddersfield police to enable her to go to Blackpool, and a permit from the Blackpool police to stay for four days. Unfortunately, she forgot to inform them when she decided to return home after only two days and was eventually fined 10/- (50p) for her forgetfulness.

Frank Dunstall, a Huddersfield man who worked as a dataller in the coalmine at Grimethorpe, found that not bothering to turn up at work could have grave consequences. He was summoned by his employer, Carlton Main Colliery Company, for absenteeism. Dunstall should have gone to work to prepare the colliery, ready for others to begin work, but failed to attend. As the company supplied the army and the navy with coal and Dunstall's absence had caused output to drop by almost 50 per cent, this was considered very serious. The magistrates fined him five pounds damages at 5/- (25p) per day but warned that any future offences by him or other miners would incur the full penalty of 16/- (80p) per day absent.

Deserters

Local magistrates had to make initial decisions with regard to the antics of any soldiers in the area. In July 1915, Aubrey Lightfoot, a 30-year-old soldier who had been in the Huddersfield hospital with a wounded hand since October 1914, was charged with being a deserter from the 3rd Battalion, the Dukes, which was then stationed at North Shields. Lightfoot declared that he had not deserted but was on sick leave, though the army disputed the medical certificate. Lightfoot then declared, not that his hand was still a problem, but that he'd been to the Front and was now suffering from tuberculosis. The magistrates didn't believe him and ordered him to be handed over to the military.

Assisting would-be deserters was also an offence that carried a penalty of a £25 fine or six months in prison. Four local ladies found themselves in court in 1915. Kate Brook of Golcar and her daughter Florrie Littlewood of Longwood had sent a set of civilian clothes to a young relative in the army in Litchfield. He was arrested and accused of being about to desert. He denied this, insisting that all he wanted to do was change units from gunnery to the signallers. It was decided that the women genuinely did not realise the seriousness of their offence as this was the first of its kind in the district, and that the young soldier did want to change units rather than desert. The women were fined £1 with 9/2d (46p) costs.

Two other women, Mary Elizabeth Roberts of Golcar and Emma Oldham of Longwood, were summoned for similar offences and also fined £1 each.

Another deserter, Herbert Mallinson Ayles, went AWOL in Ripon but returned to his home in Huddersfield. When Detective John Arthur Senior went to fetch him, he escaped out of the skylight. The police officer then gave chase across the rooftops and along the canal bank until he finally found Ayles hiding in a friend's house. Ayles still resisted arrested and the two fought before the man was finally overcome and taken to the borough police station. For his efforts in the soldier's capture Detective Senior was awarded the cost of repairs to his trousers of 15/6d (77p), rounded up to £1 as a bonus.

Detective Senior was in the news again two months later in December 1915 when a horse bolted. The driver, who was employed by the railway company, had left the horse in Victoria Lane while he went into a nearby warehouse. Unfortunately, the horse was startled when a heavy load was dropped suddenly nearby and promptly bolted, straight towards King Street and an oncoming tram.

Detective Senior heard the cries of alarm and, though he couldn't catch the horse, managed to grasp the reins and by running alongside, steered the animal away from both the tram and a motor car until he eventually pulled it to a halt. According to the *Huddersfield Chronicle* he had done a similar thing previously in 1909 when another railway horse had bolted (HC, 11 December 1915).

Ada King suffered even more because of desertion. Her son-in-law deserted from the army in April 1917. On 11 May the police arrived to search the house,

Map of Huddersfield town centre

which they did, despite being told that he'd not been there for five weeks. He was found in a cupboard. Ada was prosecuted for harbouring the man. Her defence was that he'd only arrived at midnight and that 'she'd had to suffer for her daughter'. Ada was sentenced to seven days in prison (HE, 20 May 1917).

The law also had to guard against frauds involving the army separation allowances. Dennis Stacey came from Blackpool. He was a married man and had three children but had deserted them in 1915. Though the court in Blackpool had decided he should pay 12/- (60p) a week in maintenance to his wife, he often failed to pay this and was sent to prison. After his last term in prison he was taken directly to the army recruitment office to sign up, but although he gave his wife's name as Elizabeth Stacey, he gave the address as South Street, Huddersfield, saying that he had three children and was not separated from his wife.

Part of this statement was true, but the address was false. It was the address of the woman he was living with, Elizabeth Mather.

When the case came to court, Stacey said that he'd given his address as Huddersfield to the clerk, but not mentioned anything about a separation allowance. The clerk must have filled in the form incorrectly. Although Mather did 'admit to some qualms about drawing the money' (HE, 25 April 1917), she had nevertheless continued to do so. Both were sentenced to two months in prison, with hard labour. The court had been advised that this kind of fraud was prevalent, so may have been trying to make an example of the couple.

The Munitions of War Act 1915 brought any private companies that supplied the armed forces under the control of the newly created Ministry of Munitions, which was responsible for regulating wages, hours and employment conditions as well as ensuring that orders were fulfilled quickly and properly. It was a severe offence for a worker to leave his current job at any such controlled workplace without the consent of his employer, which was often difficult to obtain. Many cases came before the magistrates of employees who wished to change employer, or who simply went to a different employer and then found themselves in trouble.

Women police

It was around this time that policing began to be seen as war work that women too could undertake as their 'feminine duty to serve the nation' (Jackson, L. A., *Women Police*). Their specific area of expertise was in dealing with women and children. Huddersfield's first lady police assistant was Edith Hoyle, a 24-year-old from Bury, Lancashire, who had been working in Blackpool as matron at a home for friendless girls. She had also been appointed probation officer there, so had considerable experience of police work and the courts. She was appointed in April 1915 on a salary of £84 per annum. The *Huddersfield Chronicle* made a brief reference on 17 April to the appointment of a 'female probation officer' to work with female offenders, which may have been a reference to Edith Hoyle.

The chief constable, John Merton, had no idea what her duties should consist of. She was left to devise her own job description as long as it included taking statements from women, dealing with children and ensuring the enforcement of the Shops Act. Her orders came directly from the chief constable or his deputy, which caused considerable ill-feeling amongst the policemen in the Borough force.

Edith had no uniform, just a badge made from the badge policemen wore on their helmets. This she pinned on the underside of her lapel. Edith was meticulous in her work, carefully studying the Shops Act and working with policemen to prosecute those who contravened it. Shops were inspected to ensure suitable toilets were provided for workers and that no unlawful goods were sold on half-day closing. On one occasion, PC Meecham went into a shop, in ordinary clothes, after closing time and was served. Waiting outside was Miss Hoyle, who returned with the constable to see the shopkeeper. He threatened both of them, saying he'd been so busy he'd just sold the goods without thinking. But the court still fined him 10/- (50p). Miss Hoyle was not always well-liked by the shopkeepers.

Another part of her job involved the Children's Act. She toured all the theatres and music halls in the area, ensuring that any children who performed there were out of the venues by nine o'clock and attended school during the day. Reports were also sent on, via the chief constable, to the next town the troupe were visiting. Children of travellers and canal workers were also investigated. Edith worked with the NSPCC but it was difficult to do anything to help the children as they moved on too quickly.

Those employing children on Saturdays found they were watched to ensure the job was not too hard for the youngsters and received a warning, followed by prosecution, if repeated. Cinemas were visited in case they allowed children to see films designated unsuitable. One manager 'took the huff' (Sharples, E. née Hoyle) but the chief constable was quick to tell him that Edith had the same authority as the men. Her comment in her autobiography was that she was 'once again ranking with the men in status but not in salary'.

She also worked on behalf of the military. Commanding officers would often write asking about the conduct of the wife on behalf of a soldier. Someone had, perhaps, written to the husband telling tales of children not being looked after. Edith would visit the women in the daytime and have a chat. The separation allowance was not much and often money had to be obtained 'by other means' (Sharples, E. née Hoyle) – presumably prostitution. Edith had a long list of homes she visited each fortnight, which was often sufficient to keep the women on the straight and narrow as any bad behaviour could see the war allowance being stopped.

Sometimes, however, she would find the house in darkness and the children crying upstairs, or find a pram parked outside a pub. Then she would go in and ensure the mother went home.

After the chief constable resigned the next man in charge, Captain Moore, would have no truck with 'women police' and refused to even speak to Edith, though when she finally resigned he was quick enough to ask, via the deputy, that she teach two policemen all she knew about the Shops Act. She refused, saying they would have to do what she had done – buy the Act and study it.

After this, Edith worked for a time at British Dyes in their police force women's section, checking the female employees in case they took to, or removed from, the works anything they shouldn't. Unfortunately the dyes affected her health and she left to return to Lancashire.

Alarming reports

In order to prevent scare-mongering, laws were passed preventing the issuing of alarming reports. One particularly harrowing report appeared, first in a Dumfries newspaper but eventually throughout the country, that a nurse, Grace Hume, who had been working in Huddersfield but had gone to the continent with a party of VADs, had not just been killed by the Germans but horrifically tortured as well. She had managed to write a note to her sister Kate describing how people were being killed and that she had had her breast cut off before dying. Another nurse had escaped and brought the letter to Kate. There was outrage at such atrocities,

Propaganda: a nurse suffering at the hands of the Germans (Taylor Library)

A Zeppelin III in flight (Taylor Library)

until it was discovered that Grace Hume was, in fact, alive and well, and had never left Huddersfield.

In 1916 a new law that people had to contend with related to drinking. Not only were hours restricted but buying drinks was affected. Joe Corrice had come over from the Isle of Man to visit his friend Walter Thornton, who he had not seen for twenty years. They ended up being the first in Huddersfield to fall foul of the new law when they decided to have a night out. Arrested for being drunk and disorderly after consuming too much rum, it was discovered that Thornton had treated Corrice to some of the drink. 'Treating' was against the new law so both were fined – Corrice 10/- (50p) for being drunk and 20/- (£1) for the drinking. Thornton was fined 40/- (£2) for providing the drink (HC, 29 January 1916).

With the fear of bombing from Zeppelins, lighting was restricted at night. It took some time before everyone fully understood the new laws but Wilfred Russell was very lucky when, yet again, he was taken before the magistrates for allowing lights to show outside his draper's shop. He'd already had a number of cautions from the police but had done little to improve the situation. Though he risked a fine of £100, he got off with just £1, plus 10/- (50p) costs. Further restrictions were put in place and enforced more strictly during the year as the Zeppelin raids extended further inland and the risk became greater. As one reached as far as Penistone, air-raid precautions were issued for the 'town to be plunged into darkness when danger threatens' (HE, 10 Feb 1916).

Employment, too, created new dangers. John Codd was summoned by the local Munitions Tribunal because he'd been smoking a pipe at work, as well as having a box of matches on him. Unfortunately, he worked at a chemical factory and his action was 'a very dangerous thing to do, putting his own and many other lives in danger'. (HE, 1 Sept 1916) As there had recently been a massive explosion at a shell factory in the north (no exact details were ever given in the newspapers, but there had been an explosion at Low Moor, Bradford in August 1916) the Tribunal fined Codd one pound, which would have been almost a week's wages.

Call-up fallout

The vast majority of men received their call-up papers with resignation and simply got on with it. Some ran away, others appealed to tribunals on various grounds, genuine or otherwise, for the right to stay at home. For others, there seemed to be only one way out.

In January 1916, John Mosby, a 55-year-old soldier from Paddock, tried to shoot himself whilst at his barracks in Hull. He was taken to the Royal Infirmary for treatment but subsequently managed to get hold of a knife and cut his throat. At the inquest his son said his father had not seemed to be depressed. In fact, John Mosby was a old soldier who had rejoined the colours in 1915 and was certainly aware of what army life could be like, so suicide was considered surprising.

In May 1916, Charles Hirst, aged 24, appealed to the Meltham Tribunal and also the East Central Tribunal at Huddersfield. Neither accepted his arguments and he was told to report for military service immediately. On 6 May his brother Edmund found him dead in the barn at their aunt's farm where both worked. The young man had locked the barn door, tied a thin rope around a beam in the roof, then round his neck. On jumping, the rope broke but was by then so tightly wrapped around Charles' neck that he was strangled to death. His aunt said that Charles was 'of a reserved disposition' (HC, 6 May 1916) and was, presumably, unable to face life in the army.

At that time, committing suicide was still considered to be a crime.

Bigamy

Although 1917 showed a record number of war marriages, not all were what they seemed. The Huddersfield and Cumberland County Northern Union football player Douglas Clark, who was a lance-corporal in the Army Service Corps, married Ann Jane Wharam on 24 January 1916. He had already had questions about their relationship, having been sent a newspaper clipping from New Zealand about a Mr and Mrs Wharam of Golcar who had been left a fortune. She'd denied this, saying it was her twin sister. Clark eventually said that if a medical examination proved she'd not had children, he would believe her. Unfortunately, the examination proved she had, in fact, had a child. Wharam then said that she'd been to Canada as a young girl and married a man called Alec Dunbar. They'd had a child but the baby had died. Clark decided he didn't want anything to do with her, because of the tales she was telling. Wharam next wrote to Clark's father, stating that she'd been married to Dunbar for two years, but then he'd told her she wasn't really married as he already had a wife living. Dunbar had eventually followed Wharam to England but died of diphtheria. Wharam found out about this via Dunbar's sister, who was also conveniently now dead.

The marriage between Clark and Wharam, under the name Jennie Wareham, had taken place in Lewisham, witnessed by Clark's father and aunt, as well as Wharam's sister, Elsie Beaumont. Elsie must have been well aware that her sister already had a husband.

Ann Jane, or Jennie, had been born Ann Jane Sykes, daughter of John and Emma Sykes. In 1906 she had married Richard Henry Wharam at Slaithwaite. The couple had three children, who at the time of the trial were aged between 8 and 2 years old. Richard Wharam had joined the army at the start of the war and was 'somewhere in France'. His wife had been drawing the separation allowance despite her involvement with Clark.

Clark managed to put the whole sorry business behind him, earning the Military Medal during his service in the army and going on to play rugby for Huddersfield again.

Excess profits tax

The government was tough on those who sought to evade paying taxes. Edwin Newman Chilton, Director of Chilton, Wrigley & Co, was prosecuted for conspiracy to defraud the Inland Revenue by not paying sufficient tax on excess profits. He wrote to a French customer, W. A. Lautermann of Le Havre, asking him to pay his account by two cheques. One would be payable to the business and the other payable to Mr Chilton, so that he could share it among the other partners without paying tax on it. The other board members did not, apparently, know what he had done. Unfortunately, he forgot about censorship. The Censor opened both letters from Lautermann, as they were coming from abroad, and so the deceit was discovered. The jury was satisfied that this was a 'one-off' offence but Chilton was still sentenced to one year in prison and ordered to pay the costs of prosecution as well as his own defence costs. (*Yorkshire Post*, 19 July 1916)

Lighting laws

Despite the fact that Huddersfield was a long way from the coast and was in little danger of bombing (although a Zeppelin did get as far as Penistone), lighting restrictions were brought in just in case.

As early as 1915, shops and business were asked to turn off all lights along the streets. This caused so much difficulty for people that it was eventually decided that lights should just be shaded (HE, 12 February 1915). Even schools had to close early during the winter terms.

Some larger firms were able to agree an exemption from these restrictions provided they had someone available at all times to take telephone calls from the authorities in the event of any Zeppelin being in the area, when the lights would immediately be doused.

On 21 June 1917, a test call was made to Messrs Robinsons at Honley. The police tried at 11.31 pm, then 11.33 pm and finally at 11.34 pm. There was no answer. When PC Varley visited the premises, Andrew Walters, working nearest the telephone, said he'd never heard it ring because he had other duties to perform that had taken him away from the area. Unfortunately for the firm this was not the first time test calls had been missed so they were fined £5.

Pigeons

Permits were required to have any kind of pigeons or even to transport them. Batley Baxter and Crowther Walker of Linthwaite were fined £2 each plus costs for keeping pigeons without a permit. Their friends, William Walker and Henry Sunderland, who had helped move the birds, got off lightly with just paying the costs of the case.

A year later a similar case caused laughter in court. Wilson Whitwam and James Wray of Golcar took their pigeons to a local show on Scapegoat Hill, where they won the homing class. When PC Webb asked to see their permits they admitted they didn't have any. Unfortunately for them the judge of the homing class was the same PC Webb and the two men ended up with a 20/- fine each. (The Worker, 15 January 1915)

Chapter Seven

Children

Looking after needy families became an important job for the local council. The Education Committee set up a sub-committee specifically to oversee arrangements for providing meals for some 'necessitous children' (HE 15 October 1914). Both breakfasts and dinners were provided for six days of the week, excluding Sunday, and the Aspley Cookery Centre was expanded to include a kitchen to produce the meals.

By December 1915, twenty-seven teachers and three clerks were in the army. Fifteen teachers, two clerks, four attendance officers and three caretakers had attested under the Derby Scheme. Twenty-three teachers and one clerk had been rejected as unfit, mainly on account of eyesight.

Teachers and pupils regularly contributed towards war charities. One enterprising group (Kathleen Walker, Phyllis Marsden, Dorothy Hollis and Guy Aspinall), from the Higher Elementary School in Hillhouse, made dolls' clothes as well as dressing some dolls for sale, raising 13/6d (63p) for the Belgian Relief Fund (HE, 29 December 2014). Another group (Doris Gledhill, Eliza Peckett, Edith Dyson, Alice and Margaret Livesey) put their own pocket money towards buying cigarettes for all the soldiers who had enlisted from their Sunday School. One of the soldiers, Private A. Ingleby, wrote to the *Huddersfield Examiner* in order to thank the children publicly.

Other schools took more direct action to help the war effort. A Cadets Corps was formed at King James' School in Almondbury, to which more than half of the schoolboys belonged, wearing a khaki uniform and drilling with much enthusiasm.

Schoolrooms were also being lent free of charge for drilling by the local Voluntary Corps or for various committee meetings for raising funds. Thousands of leaflets about the war and economy of food issued by the Board of Education were distributed through the schools.

Juvenile crime

One recurring theme in the magistrates court was that of juvenile crime. The police force had been drastically reduced as many of its officers had previously been in the army and were called up immediately in 1914. Added to this, it was felt that family life was unstable as the 'man of the house' was often away and children therefore lacked his discipline. On 5 February 1916, the *Huddersfield Chronicle* ran a story about the 'Clutching Hand' gang – a group of youngsters aged from 7 to 13, who had perpetrated a series of thefts in the area. Six boys (aged between 7 and 13) and two girls (both aged 11) had stolen a box of cigarettes. The shopkeeper, Lewis Lodge, said he had previously seen children hanging around and then missed small amounts of cigars, cigarettes and matches. Another boy had seen the gang leaving the shop, followed them and watched them share out the cigarettes. The lad promptly took the box and as many of the cigarettes as he could from the gang and returned them to the shop.

The leader of the gang was a boy aged 7, who was already known to the police for having been involved in the theft of a tricycle but had not been prosecuted because of his age. The chief constable informed the court that there were numerous charges against the children, including theft of candles, clothing and matches. The children all admitted the thefts and were placed on probation for two years. The probation officer, T. Grundy, pointed out that the name of the gang and bad behaviour, seemed to have come from films shown at the pictures that 'had an adverse influence' on the children, and asked the magistrates to include a ban on going to the pictures for the duration of the probation, which the magistrates agreed to. The film was probably *Exploits of Elaine*, an adventure story released in a series of chapters over the course of a few weeks. The villain of the piece was known as The Clutching Hand.

Crosland Moor Workhouse

Just a short while later on 19 February, the same newspaper had another story of yet more children in the gang. Three boys stole a pocket knife from Woolworths and again they were put on probation for two years and prohibited from visiting the picture house during that time. One 9-year-old boy was committed to Barnes Home, Heaton Mersey near Manchester, which was an 'industrial school' set up to provide training for destitute children, until he was 16 years old. However, the boy's father appealed against this sentence. The man had been wounded and invalided home so would be able to look after the boy. The magistrates agreed to sentence the lad in the same way as the rest of the gang.

Neglect of children

Whether the men being away from home made any difference to the number of cases of neglect seen is not known, but an example of how this was handled is shown by Annie Senior of Moldgreen, whose case for neglect was reported in the *Huddersfield Chronicle* in February 1916. Her husband was away on active service, she received a separation allowance of 25/- (£1.25) per week. She was visited by Dr Gill, who was one of the female medical officers in the district.

Her baby had weighed over 9lb at birth in March 1915, but a few weeks later this had reduced to 6lb. Four of the mother's previous children had died from 'wasting' and all had scabies. The whole house was dirty and neglected. Annie was given a month's supply of dried milk for the baby and in April the whole family had been taken to the sanatorium to be disinfected. By June the house and family were again in a dirty and neglected condition. This time Dr Moore, the medical officer, called round and found the baby being given just water. The child was thin and 'flea bitten'. The situation was left a further eight weeks to 'see if it improved'. Despite further regular visits by the health workers, nothing changed. Annie was seen going into the cinema at 9 pm with the baby in a shawl, having left a 5-year-old at home looking after another baby, aged 2. When asked why the baby was being fed only half-cream milk, Annie said she couldn't afford full-cream, despite the fact that the doctor could clearly see a kitten lapping at what appeared to be full-cream milk (though nothing was said about how he could see the difference). The medical officers decided there was a serious risk to the little girl if left, and asked the magistrates for a removal order. The baby was taken into Crosland Moor Workhouse for six months, after which she would be returned to the family, presumably in strong enough health to be able to withstand the situation.

Huddersfield Day Nursery

After nearly two years of war, it was recognised that if women were able to take the place of men at work, provision had to be made for their children. Previously the argument against a nursery was that it might 'set mothers free from their parental responsibilities' (HE, 6 October 1916). The National Association for the Prevention of Infant Mortality and for the Welfare of Infants wrote to the mayor suggesting a day nursery was now a matter of necessity, provided, of course, that it was 'properly conducted and controlled'. Early in the year funds had been raised, thanks, it was said, to Mrs Blamires, the mayoress, who 'had a magic way of getting money when they needed it'. With the help of some government grants a nursery for twenty-five children was opened on Queen Street. Huddersfield was seen as one of the pioneer towns for its work to improve the lives of babies in the area.

National Baby Week 1917

Even before the war, infant mortality had been a problem. In December 1914, the schools had had to close for eight weeks to try and prevent the spread of measles, which had already killed nineteen children. With so many adult casualties from the fighting, the country began to realise that action must be taken to look after the children and ensure an increasing survival rate. It was decided to have National Baby Week in the first week of July in order to enlighten public opinion on the importance of mothers and children. Churches had sermons on maternity and child welfare and talks on childcare were given to meetings in schools throughout the district.

Some of the advertising posters suggested that it was more dangerous to be a baby in England than a soldier in France. One letter to the *Huddersfield Examiner* compared death rates in the UK of 102 per 1,000 to New Zealand's 50 per 1,000. Huddersfield was just above the national average at 104 per 1,000. The writer went on to comment that 'those too poor to raise children have too many and those wealthy enough choose not to because of the cost'. The writer even wanted to publish a list of those with no children or only one. 'What a theme for shirkers' week,' he said (HE, 2 July 1917).

Nestlé's advertising campaign to 'save the babies' suggested they were more likely to survive if using their milk instead of breast feeding. They even offered, for the first 10,000 applicants only, an album of *Heroes All*, showing men now in the forces who had been raised on tinned milk. It does not say how many applicants actually applied for the photo album.

In Huddersfield the first event was a massive garden party in Greenhead Park. Invitations were sent out to over 1,000 mothers of babies under 12 months old and special cars provided from tram termini to the park gates. Music was provided by the Lindley Prize Brass Band and a tent was set up for the Huddersfield Day Nursery, which was quite an innovation at the time. There were no competitions, just informal talks to spread information and, perhaps, to form self-help groups. An important visitor was Benjamin Broadbent, who had been mayor of Huddersfield in 1904 and was known as 'the godfather of infant

Bandstand, Greenhead Park

welfare' because of his work in raising the standard of child care.

The feeling was that parents had a duty to look after their children as well as they possibly could since the population had been decimated by the war and a new generation was needed, but the municipal councils also had a 'duty to give the children a chance of happiness' by providing play areas, wide streets, good housing, and welfare support (HE, 6 July 1917).

Workers

By 1917 the government was beginning to realise that working children did not get a good education. They proposed ending the half-time system, whereby children could work part-time and go to school part-time, a system that neither teachers nor employers really liked. It was also suggested that youngsters at work who were sent to college for training should have this time included in their total working hours – the forerunner of 'day release'. The school leaving age was to be raised to 14, though none of this was implemented until 1918. During the war years it was perfectly acceptable for children to work as much as thirty-three hours a week, in addition to their time at school (van Emden and Humphries). However, a watchful eye was kept on them. Taylor, Livesey & Co Ltd were fined for employing a number of youngsters under 16 without having medical certificates for them. Their excuse was that the young people were girls and they didn't realise that the law requiring medical certificates applied to girls too.

The local industries were not the only place children were expected to help the war effort. Since the import of raw materials was so difficult, as much as possible was grown in England, including flax. When this was due to be harvested, boy scouts were asked to volunteer to spend a week in the fields. The Huddersfield group camped in Sherburn-in-Elmet, where their working day lasted from morning until mid afternoon, when they could take part in football and cricket matches against other scout groups. Swimming and cycling around the Selby and York areas were also popular activities, with a concert each Friday for those leaving on the Saturday. Huddersfield Scout master Frank Beever asked in the *Huddersfield Examiner* on 13 August 1918 for more volunteer scoutmasters to come and help. He described life there as being run on military lines. Everyone was assigned to a 'patrol'. The camp was guarded day and night, whilst another patrol would act as orderlies to keep the camp tidy.

Chapter Eight

Short shrift

Wartime don'ts

The National Organising Committee for War Savings decided to help everyone 'do their bit' by issuing a list of ways in which to make further savings and help the war effort. Not using a motor car or motorcycle seem fairly obvious. Every bit of petrol was needed, so essential use only was allowed. But people were exhorted not to buy new clothes either, or to be ashamed of wearing old clothes in wartime so that cloth could be made into uniforms or bandages. One wartime 'don't' was directed specifically at the better off – don't keep more servants than are really needed. This would not only save money but would set the right example in freeing labour for more useful (i.e. fighting) purposes.

New from old

Raw material shortage made it necessary to recycle fabric wherever possible. Originally sold off to dealers, now the government sent old uniforms direct to the mills where those that were wearable were cleaned and revamped before being sent back. Ones in too bad a state had the buttons and badges removed, then were shredded, turned into yarn and made into blankets.

Paper became both more expensive and scarcer. Vegetable parchment from Germany for the production of paper obviously ceased. But esparto grass, also used to make paper, which had been imported from North Africa and the Mediterranean countries or from wood pulp from Scandinavia, became difficult to obtain because of the increased activity of German U-boats. Shipping rates also increased from around 5/- (25p) before the war to around 40/- (£2) per ton. Supplies of wood pulp and bleaching chemicals were requisitioned by the government to replace cotton in the manufacture of explosives. The government also took over many of the railway trucks for military use, thus making transport even more difficult. Printing was not a reserved occupation, therefore the workforce dwindled. Retailers were advised not to wrap goods in paper and to economise on the use of paper bags.

The *Huddersfield Examiner* began advertising for the return of old newspapers and magazines in good condition, giving 1/- (5p) per 14lb (6.35kg) bundle (HE, 1 August 1917). In addition, the number of pages printed was reduced and the price increased to one penny.

Food shortages

The effects of the German blockade caused serious concern that Britain would not be able to feed itself if the war continued. People were asked to reduce their consumption of bread and eat up all their crusts, though many bakers objected to the fact that there was no restriction of the amount of beer that could be bought (beer also needed grain). Different flours were used and additives, such as peas or beans, helped to make the grain go further.

Everyone was asked to do their bit to grow food or use it more effectively. Every spare scrap of land could be planted out to grow broad beans, peas, turnips or swedes to use instead of potatoes or even instead of meat. Allotments sprang up everywhere and the council arranged for a lecturer from Leeds University, Mr A. S. Galt, to come and give lectures in the Town Hall about 'Gardening in War Time'. The council also bought seed potatoes in bulk, selling them at cost to allotment holders and even the land near the drill hall, used for training, was partially dug up for potatoes.

Although rationing was not in force at first, most people seem to have voluntarily cut back and eaten less during the war. Bakers decided not to produce hot cross buns during Easter, as these were seen as a luxury item, and baconless days became the norm as supplies of bacon from Denmark, Sweden and Holland dwindled. Any bacon that reached Britain was frequently requisitioned by the army as the soldiers' needs had to come first.

As starvation became a greater threat, Huddersfield Food Control Committee took the step of commandeering margarine from shops in the district, and took over all deliveries. To buy the margarine a ration card had to be produced. Later everyone had to register with a butcher in order to claim their meat rations – 5oz (0.14kg) meat (including bone) per person per week. Some meats were rationed by price, some by weight so one coupon might buy 5d-worth (3p) of uncooked meat or 12oz (0.34kg) poultry or a meat meal at a café.

Teashops and cafés became rationed by law as to how much they could sell – no crumpets, muffins or any other 'fancy' breads; no cakes with more than 15 per cent sugar (normally this would be around 30 per cent), and no more than 2oz (0.056 kg) cakes or bread per customer.

Everyone was not just encouraged to grow food but advised on how to make the best use of it. Children needed to 'get a fair amount of fat daily' including dripping, suet, butter, bacon as well as fresh fruit and vegetables (HE, 7 May 1917), but three meals a day was quite sufficient, with nothing in between. Sugar was not needed at all. Cookery demonstrations were held in church halls and schools and at mothers' meetings, where suitable recipes were distributed.

The Board of Agriculture asked farmers to increase their production of pigs and poultry as well as ploughing up more grassland, though this request was not always fulfilled. The Ramsden Estate, which owned a large amount of farmland in the area, refused to allow the Almondbury & District Farmers Association to change their grassland to corn (HC, 13 February 1915). The association then wrote to the local MP, Mr Sherwell, to ask him to try to put pressure on the Ramsden Estate to allow their tenant farmers to plant corn.

Often, though, the land was not really suitable for the crops sown, being thick turf just ploughed and not having enough fertiliser. Lectures were held to advise farmers on how to get the best out of their land and how to manage crops, such as oats, which they had never grown before.

Unfortunately, despite their best efforts the yield was still low. The West Riding War Agricultural Committee did what it could to help by supplying seeds and fertiliser, providing new, up-to-date machinery or teams of horses with skilled handlers as well as trying to obtain exemptions from call-up for farmworkers.

Even pets were on short rations. It was forbidden to feed dogs with meat or bread scraps that could feed humans. In 1915, one butcher was complaining that cat meat had not only increased in price but was becoming scarce because all the horses had been sent to the war (HE, 2 July 1915).

Horse flesh as beef

As well as food being in short supply, some people were not averse to mislabelling goods. Charles William Taylor, a butcher in Beast Market, was summoned to court for keeping horse meat for sale, although he had not been registered for the purpose. This was the first case of its kind in Huddersfield, though the prosecution was keen to stress that they 'were not attempting to belittle the value of horse flesh as human food … people should know what they were buying' (HE, 17 December 1917). Taylor had been selling the meat as lean beef and for pie meat, making a good profit since horse meat was generally around 7d (3p) per pound, whereas beef was 1/4d (6p). Taylor's defence was that the meat was for his own consumption, as he ran a lodging house with eight or nine lodgers, but eventually admitted that he had sold the meat and was fined £20. The newspaper commented that this was a 'crime against the poorest class of people'.

National kitchens

Since cooking on a large scale cut down on the need for fuel and allowed bulk-buying savings, the government decided to set up national kitchens where large amounts of basic food could be produced and sold more or less at cost to anyone who wanted, or needed, it. Since many women were now part of the workforce, this was a godsend and became very popular, though the menu was rather limited.

In Huddersfield the first national kitchen was opened in Aspley in July 1918. There was nowhere to sit so meals had to be taken away. A full meal costing around 8d (4p) might include a Cornish pasty, vegetables, rice and pudding such

Milton Church

as jam roll or ginger pudding and custard.

At the sale of work at Milton Church in 1917, booklets were sold entitled *War Time Cookery and Economy Hints* (KC1006/2/12/2/6). This gave lots of recipes for use with a hay box to save fuel. Bacon joints could be boiled for forty minutes, then left overnight in the box and potatoes only needed two minutes boiling plus two hours in the box. This was probably quite good advice as many women workers must have welcomed such methods of saving housework. The domestic economy advice was a little dubious when it recommended soaking a piece of coke in paraffin to use as a firelighter. An alternative was a piece of asbestos, also soaked in paraffin, then fastened on a stout wire, to be re-used as often as required. Keeping boots and shoes dry and making them last longer could easily be done, apparently, by brushing the soles with boiled linseed oil, to which petrol or benzene had been added.

To save the cost of a chimney sweep, just putting ½lb saltpetre on the fire once a month was recommended as the fumes would clear the chimney of soot. Saltpetre, as well as being a preservative for meat, is a component of gunpowder and can give off toxic fumes in a fire.

Chapter Nine

Coming to an end

Though millions from all over the world died during the war, the 1918 influenza epidemic claimed even more lives. Called Spanish Flu because it was believed that it was more virulent there than anywhere else, though its origin was variously reported as being USA or the forces hospital in Etaples. Schools were closed from June right through the winter as so many staff and children were absent. Mills and factories had difficulty continuing work as workers were off sick. People were advised to avoid all large groups, such as theatres, churches, schools, music halls and so on, and even the hospital stopped all visiting. Trains and trams were advised to keep windows open at all times, and were running reduced timetables because of the number of staff off. Eucalyptus oil spread on handkerchiefs was suggested as a preventive. Soldiers on leave were banned from attending theatres and concerts in order to try to keep them safe from the dreaded disease.

In July 1918, twelve deaths were reported in Huddersfield in one week, one of which was a soldier who had only just arrived home on leave. Many soldiers who survived the war succumbed to the flu epidemic, which lasted, on-and-off, until 1920.

The celebrations for Huddersfield's jubilee year took place in 1918. A plaque was put up in the Town Hall commemorating all past mayors and town clerks and ten jubilee scholarships were established.

The local political situation was changing too. The Representation of the Peoples Act 1918 had almost trebled the number of parliamentary voters and, for the local government voting, women outnumbered men for the first time. Despite the restrictions on women's entitlement to vote, it was a step in the right direction. The first general election after this extension of the franchise was to take place in December 1918, just a few weeks after the end of the war.

While much has been said about the number of men who died, millions did actually return. Many physically injured, many more mentally disturbed by the years of fighting. At home too, life had changed. More women had tasted the freedom of working, earning a wage, being independent. Others had found their lifestyle diminished as the breadwinner was killed or no longer able to hold down a well-paid job.

The government had taken over or legislated about almost every aspect of life in Britain. Men returned to their pre-war jobs, ousting the women who had 'held the fort' for the past four years. Unfortunately, life did not just return to normal.

Britain had amassed millions of war debts, lost export markets, and high inflation exacerbated a dire economic situation.

Social effects

Venereal disease had always been a problem for troops (almost 500,000 troops were treated for various forms of VD according to the World War One centenary website), but it became more critical during the war. In 1916 it became a crime for women to solicit men in uniform and later laws brought in the infamous powers for police to forcibly examine any woman suspected of having a VD. As the war drew to an end it was realised that action was needed. The Huddersfield branch of the National Council for Combating Venereal Disease held a meeting in the Town Hall on 9 October 1918, which was so well-attended that not everyone could get into the building. The speakers commented that they had been trying for over two years to raise support so hoped that this would now be forthcoming. Though they did admit that the subject was the responsibility of both men and women, the blame was targeted at 'flappers' – young women (actually girls between 14 and 18) who supposedly flung themselves at anyone in uniform. The NCCVD suggested that these girls needed both sympathy and support from private clinics, but the causes could also be attributed to bad and overcrowded housing, lack of teaching about the subject of sexual hygiene, and the 'intemperance' of the girls as they often had the money to buy drink as they hadn't done previously. There were over seventy meetings planned for the area, so the subject was obviously of great concern.

A few days later, the National Union of Women Workers discussed the subject and heard a report from Miss Irving about the 'patrol sub-committee', which oversaw women patrolling the streets in the hope of meeting and talking to the girls. They had already had some success in 're-directing' some girls, but also gained much insight into their situation.

Huddersfield decided to set up special clinics at the infirmary to help those suffering the disease and appointed a lady doctor.

Armistice

By November the newspapers were full of armistices being signed or asked for by various central powers. Bulgaria had already agreed an armistice at the end of September, Turkey agreed its armistice on 30 October, Austria on 3 November and on 9 November, the German Kaiser abdicated, followed by the Austrian Kaiser two days later. On 11 November, the armistice between Germany and the Allies was signed, though the war did not formally end until 28 June 1919 with the signing of the Treaty of Versailles.

There was rejoicing all over the country and everywhere people were asking

'Is it true?' Outside the Examiner office a notice was posted as soon as the news was received, just before 11 am on 11 November. The Union Flag was flown from the Town Hall for the first time in four years and from the windows, people hung out the flags of the Allies – the Stars and Stripes of America, the French Tricolour and the black, yellow and red of Belgium. Anyone who had flags was out on the streets waving them and cheering. The *Huddersfield Examiner* did, however, comment that there was also a 'quiet joy' and a 'sense of relief' rather than over ecstatic joy, as many remembered the loss of life too. 'It was an occasion on which to weep with those that weep or to rejoice with those that rejoiced.' (HE, 11 November 1918)

The local courts had a general amnesty for anyone due to appear that day, work ceased in the factories, trams stopped and shops closed. Church bells rang, also for the first time in four years.

There was a definite sense of a new world order coming – there had been revolutions in Russia, the Austro-Hungarian empire had broken up into many different countries, and republics had been declared across Europe.

Instead of the planned 'guns week' to raise money for more weapons, the week was designated a 'thanksgiving week', still raising money but this time for reconstruction to change the war industries to peace industries. There would be no immediate discharge of munitions workers but anyone who wanted to leave could do so. Overtime stopped immediately and hours of work were reduced.

Memorials

How to provide suitable memorials to those killed in the war had been discussed almost from the start. The Anglo-South African War had only ended in 1902, after which a statue, known as the 'Fallen Heroes', was erected in Greenhead Park and unveiled by Sir John French, a commander of the BEF in the Great War. The men who died then were buried thousands of miles away and so services were held each year on the anniversary of this unveiling, 20 May.

As the Great War, which should have ended at Christmas 1914, approached its first anniversary, a service of intercession

Fallen Heroes Memorial, Greenhead Park

Intercession Day

In every Church and Chapel to-morrow prayers will be offered for the Victory of our soldiers, and a collection made for the relief and comfort of our sick and wounded at the front.

If you are unable to attend Church or Chapel to-morrow send your donation direct to
BRITISH RED CROSS SOCIETY & THE ORDER OF ST. JOHN,
Room 99 – 83, Pall Mall, London, S.W.

Intercession Day notice

had been held in St George's Square. Organised by the mayor, Joseph Blamires, to remember a 'year of the most devastating and costly war the country has ever known' (HE, 9 August 1915), thousands attended the service led by a choir of 500. The band of the 5th Battalion West Riding Regiment led a procession from the Town Hall to the square and played the usual hymns of remembrance – *Oh God Our Help in Ages Past, Abide with Me, Eternal Father Strong to Save* – and finished with the national anthem.

In 1917 a 'celebration' was held in St George's Square at which 'Huddersfield recorded its inflexible determination to continue to a victorious end' (HE, 7 August 1917). By that time the general feeling seems to have been that there was no alternative but to fight on. It was also commented in the newspaper that

Huddersfield had contributed around £140,000 and between 10,000 and 15,000 men to the war.

Many small memorials were put up during the war. A stained glass window was set up in July 1918 in St Bartholomew's Church in Marsden to commemorate those already fallen, with a plaque to be added after the war with all the names of those from the parish who had died. The window was paid for by James Whitehead, who lived in Oldham but was originally from Marsden.

The service held in August 1918 was the first one to be specifically named as 'Remembrance Day'.

Held in the parish church in Huddersfield the vicar, Canon Tupper-Carey commented on the previous services. The first, he said, had been to pray for the spirit of endurance, the second for unity of spirit and effort, the third for the 'glorious realisation of the fellowship of the free nations in a crusade against the

St Peter's Church, Huddersfield

tyranny of force', while this fourth one would be for the rekindling of hope and confidence in the future (HE, 6 August 1918). It was becoming obvious that the war would be ending soon but no one could tell exactly when.

The actual fighting took place far away and many wanted the bodies of their boys brought home, though few could afford it, even if they knew which battlefield their menfolk had originally been buried in. Those who did know where their relative was buried at least wanted to put a memorial stone on the place. The government refused to allow this, saying that all graves were marked with a wooden cross. If any were damaged in the fighting, they would be replaced as soon as it was safe to do so. The promise was that, after the war, all graves would have a suitable stone. Henry Walker of the Army Service Corps, whose

War Memorial, Greenhead Park

family lived in Slaithwaite, wrote to the newspaper to say he had visited the grave of his brother, G. W. Q. Walker, who had been killed in July 1916. He re-assured everyone that the cemetery and graves were well-cared for by the local population. He also referred to the grave of Captain C. O. Denham-Jubb, who had been killed at the very start of the war in August 1914. 'It says much for the care that is bestowed upon it, that it should look so nice three and a half years later.' (HE, 31 January 1918)

In 1919 Leigh Tolson donated Ravensknowle Park to Huddersfield Corporation to use as a museum to commemorate his two nephews who had been killed in the war, and villages around the town set up their own memorials.

One thing everyone was agreed on was that a lasting memorial should be provided in Huddersfield, though many felt it should support the living rather than just be a memorial to the dead. The War Memorial Committee, headed by Sir William Raynor, had initial plans to raise £100,000, but they had to be curtailed in the light of economic depression that existed after the war. Instead over £50,000 was obtained. Only part of this was spent on the memorial in Greenhead Park. The rest was invested with a view to providing extra income for the infirmary.

In April 1924, the memorial was finally ready. There was no ornamental carving on the memorial, nor long-winded inscriptions, just a simple 'In Memoriam 1914-1918' on the column of victory with its bronze sacrificial cross.

The procession began, as usual, in front of the Town Hall, led by the band and drums of 5th Battalion Duke of Wellington's Regiment (West Riding). Representatives of other local battalions, as well as representatives from all of the armed services took part, together with local old comrades' associations, volunteer groups of nurses and motorists, boy scouts and parties from every kind of committee that had been formed during the war, all marched up to Greenhead Park, along with various officials of Huddersfield Borough, the architect of the memorial, Sir Charles Nicholson, and mayors from Huddersfield, Bradford, Dewsbury, Halifax and Brighouse. Relatives of the fallen were given special places near the front.

General Sir Charles Harington inspected the guard-of-honour and men from Beckett's Park Hospital (Leeds) who also attended. Surprisingly, amongst the wounded soldiers were men from the mental hospital at Kirkburton, who were also introduced to the general.

Later the general unveiled the memorial and prayers were led by the Vicar of Huddersfield, Canon Tupper-Carey, followed by the *Last Post*, one minute's silence and *Reveille*, a sequence that would become traditional in the future. Over 4,500 men from Huddersfield had died during the four years of war plus thousands of others injured physically and mentally.

Memorials and rolls of honour were set up in working men's clubs, churches, schools and other public buildings, though many of these have now been lost or are in very poor condition.

Eventually the Imperial War Graves Commission (now Commonwealth War Graves Commission, CWGC) provided funds for a cross of sacrifice in major towns and cities, such as the one in Edgerton Cemetery.

War Memorial, Edgerton Cemetery

Abroad, gravestones were provided by the CWGC, which insisted all should be alike. Many towns in France and Belgium have war cemeteries and war memorials that include those from local Huddersfield battalions.

Tyne Cot cemetery, Belgium

War Memorial, Arras, France

Menin Gate, Belgium

The Menin Gate was built as a memorial to those whose last resting place is unknown.

Timeline for the war

1914

June

On 28 June, Archduke Franz Ferdinand, the heir to the throne of the Austro-Hungarian Empire, and his wife Sophie, are assassinated in Sarajevo, Bosnia by Serbian Gavrilo Princep.

Archduke Franz Ferdinand and his wife Sophie (Taylor Library)

July

Austria-Hungary sends troops to the Serbian frontier and Serbia immediately mobilises its own troops. Backed by its allies, Germany, Austria-Hungary declares war on Serbia. Austria bombs the Serbian capital, Belgrade. Some German patrols cross the French border.

August
French troops mobilise. Germany declares war on Russia, France and Belgium. Italy and United States announce neutrality. Britain tries to organise a conference to avoid war, but this is not taken up by Germany. Germany enters Belgium, a neutral country. Britain issues an ultimatum to Germany. When this is not complied with, Britain declares war on Germany.

Royal Navy cruiser HMS Amphion is sunk by German mines. The first British troops, the 'Old Contemptibles', land in France, comprising mainly regulars and reservists, quickly followed volunteers who responded to the 'Your King and Country Need You' campaign. German troops occupy Belgium. Nearly 9,000 British troops die at the Battle of Le Cateau.

September
First Battle of the Marne.

October
The First Battle of Ypres. Turkey forms an alliance with Germany and enters the war.

November
Trench warfare begins. The western front is lined with trenches on both sides. The British enter Basra to ensure a safe supply of oil for the Royal Navy.

December
Battle of the Falkland Islands. Three German cruisers are destroyed by the Royal Navy. The east coast of Britain is bombed by the German navy, killing 137 civilians in Scarborough, Whitby and Hartlepool.

1915

January
Zeppelins bomb Great Yarmouth and King's Lynn, killing five civilians. This is the first airborne attack on Britain.

February
German U-boats blockade Britain, attacking any vessels, even those from neutral countries. Allied navies bomb the Dardanelles and Gallipoli.

March
The British Offensive at Neuve Chapelle begins, resulting in very high Allied losses. This exposes what became known as 'The Shell Crisis', suggesting that British shells were poor quality and in short supply.

April
Second Battle of Ypres, when Germany used poison gas for the first time. The Allies landed 70,000 troops from France, Britain and the Commonwealth, at Gallipoli.

May
Almost 1,200 lives are lost when a German U-boat torpedoes the British liner Lusitania. Among them are 128 Americans. This created a US-German diplomatic crisis. London suffers its first Zeppelin raid, when seven people are killed. In Parliament, a coalition government is formed.

August
Although the Allies land troops at Suvla Bay, Gallipoli, they are unable to move off the beaches because of action by the Turkish troops. Whitehaven is attacked by a German U-boat.

October
The Germans execute British nurse Edith Cavell because she helped POWs escape from Belgium. She becomes a martyr and British heroine.

December
Sir Douglas Haig replaces Sir John French as Commander in Chief of the British

The Lusitania

Expeditionary Force (BEF). Allied troops begin the evacuation of Gallipoli, completed in January the following year.

1916

January
The British Government passes the Military Service Act, introducing conscription, which became law on 25 May.

February
The Battle of Verdun begins, lasting ten months, with the loss of over a million men.

March
Germany and Austria declare war on Portugal.

April
The Allies fail in their attempt to relieve the garrison at Kut in Mesopotamia. The garrison is forced to surrender and 3,000 British and 6,000 Indian troops are taken captive. Most of these die of disease and starvation in appalling conditions in prison camps.

May
Battle of Jutland, Britain and Germany both lose six ships.

June
HMS Hampshire is mined off Orkney, with the loss of Lord Kitchener as well as 643 crewmen and general staff.

July
The Battle of the Somme on 1 July sees the highest casualties in one day's fighting in British military history. Almost 60,000 Allied soldiers died, were wounded or missing.

August
Italy declares war on Germany.

September
The first Zeppelin is shot down over mainland Britain. The British capture Ginchy, a place of strategic importance, because of its excellent view of the Somme battlefield. Tanks are used for the first time in the Battle of Flers-Courcelette and play a vital role in winning the Battle of Thiepval.

FEARED LOSS OF LORD KITCHENER.

MISSING WITH STAFF FROM SUNKEN WARSHIP.

H.M.S. HAMPSHIRE MINED OR TORPEDOED ON THE WAY TO RUSSIA.

ADMIRALTY OFFICIAL.

The following telegram has been received from the Commander-in-Chief of the Grand Fleet at 10-30 this morning :—

I have to report with deep regret that H.M.S. Hampshire (Captain Herbt. John Savill, R.N.), with Lord Kitchener and his Staff on board, was sunk last night, about 8 p.m., to the west of the Orkneys, either by mine or torpedo.

Four boats were seen by observers on shore to leave the ship. The wind was north north-west, and heavy seas were running.

Patrol vessels and destroyers at once proceeded to the spot, and a party was sent along the coast to search, but only some bodies and a capsized boat have been found up to the present.

As the whole shore has been searched from the seaward I greatly fear that there is little hope of there being any survivors.

No report has yet been received from the search parties on shore.

H.M.S. Hampshire was on her way to Russia.

H.M.S. Hampshire was an armoured cruiser with a displacement of 10,850 tons, and an indicated horse-power of 21,508. She was completed in 1905, and carried a crew of 655 men. She carried four 7.5 inch guns, six 6 inch, twenty 3-pounders, and 2 machine guns. She was fitted with two torpedo tubes. Her speed was 23·47 knots.

December
David Lloyd George is elected as British Prime Minister. Germany delivers a Peace Note to the Allies hoping to reach a compromise. The Battle of Verdun ends.

1917

January
Germany tries to starve Britain into submission by continuing it blockade and submarine warfare.

This causes the US to cut diplomatic relations with Germany because of the threat to its own shipping. The Zimmermann telegram was intercepted by British intelligence, revealing that Germany was inciting Mexico to attack the US.

February
The Germans begin to pull troops back to secure the Hindenburg Line. The Turks retreat to Baghdad.

March
The beginning of the Russian revolution means more German troops are available to fight on the western front. The British successfully capture Baghdad.

April
The US declares war on Germany and begins an immediate mobilisation of troops. At the Battle of Arras, Britain uses new tactics, such as 'creeping barrages', which prove successful.

June
The Battle of Messines Ridge. The British successfully take the ridge with very few casualties. They had detonated 19 mines under the German front lines just prior to the battle. The explosions are said to have been heard from England. Germans launch the first major bomber raid on London. 162 people are killed with 432 injured. First US troops arrive in France.

October
Phase three of the Ypres Offensive begins. British and French troops take Poelcapelle, but as there is heavy rain over the next two days, the battlefield turns to mud. The battle for Passchendaele begins.

November
The British capture Gaza. The Battle of Cambrai begins. The Royal Flying Corps

are used to drop bombs on German anti-tank guns to clear a path for the Allied tanks and troops. The Battle of Passchendaele ends with half a million casualties in gaining five miles of land.

December
The British liberate Jerusalem.

1918

March
Soviet Russia agrees its own peace with Germany and her allies. The German 'Spring Offensive' begins, using 'Stormtrooper' units which shatter the British positions near St Quentin in France and take 16,000 British prisoners. A massive air battle between 70 aircraft takes place over the Somme.

April
The Allies try to block the harbours at Ostend and Zeebrugge by destroying old vessels in the harbour entrances. The plan works at Zeebrugge but fails at Ostend.

May
The second British attack on Ostend is successful when. HMS Vindictive is scuttled in the harbour, preventing German usage of the port.

July
The second Battle of the Marne is the last phase of the German Spring Offensive. Allied counter attacks inflict terrible casualties on the Germans. The defeat means cancelling the planned Invasion of Flanders and puts the Germans on the defensive.

September
The Battle of St Quentin; British and American troops launch devastating offensives breaking the Hindenburg Line along the Canal Du Nord and St Quentin Canal.

October
A German and Austrian peace proposal is sent to the American President, Woodrow Wilson, requesting an armistice. The whole of the west Flanders coast is liberated by the Allies. Sailors of the German High Seas Fleet at Jade mutiny and refuse to leave harbour to attack the British Fleet. The Turkish army surrenders to the British in Mesopotamia. Turkey signs an armistice with the Allies and fighting ceases.

November
German sailors mutiny at Kiel. Austria-Hungary signs an armistice with the Allies. Armistice negotiations between the Allies and Germany begin. Kaiser Wilhelm abdicates and goes to Holland. Armistice Day: November 11th. The Armistice is signed at 5.00am and comes into effect at 11.00am.

1919

28 June – exactly five years after the assassination of Archduke Franz Ferdinand, the Treaty of Versailles brings a formal end to the war.

Bibliography

Barham, Peter. (2004) *Forgotten Lunatics of the Great War,* Yale University Press

Brook, Anne C. (2009) *God, Grief & Community: Commemoration of the Great War in Huddersfield*, unpublished PhD thesis, University of Leeds

Clapham, Marcus (selector) (2009), *The Wordsworth Book of First World War Poetry*, Wordsworth Editions Ltd

Colley, R. (2013), *World War One: History in an Hour*, Harper Press

Free, L. F. (1996), *Royds Hall*, L. F. Free as school booklet

Haigh, E. A. H. (ed) (1992), *Huddersfield, A Most Handsome Town*, Kirklees Cultural Services

Haythornthwaite, Philip J.(1992), *The World War One Source Book*, Cassell plc

Hayward, J.(2002), *Myths and Legends of the First World War*, Sutton Publishing Ltd

Heath, C.(2004), *Denby & District II*, Wharncliffe Books

Jackson, Louise A.(2006), *Women Police: Gender, Welfare and Surveillance in the Twentieth Century,* Manchester University Press

Littlewood, A.(2003), *Storthes Hall Remembered,* University of Huddersfield

Lockwood, Ernest. (1936), *Colne Valley Folk,* Heath Cranton Ltd

Minter, G. & E.(1995 - 2002), *Discovering Old Huddersfield, Parts One to Five*, H. Barden & Company

Pearce, Cyril. (2001), *Comrades in Conscience*, Francis Boutle

Roberts, A.(2012), *Love, Tommy: Letters Home from the Great War*, Imperial War Museum

Sharples, E. (née Hoyle) (1968), *My Life's Work*, unpublished manuscript, Bury Central Library

Stevenson, D.(2004), *1914-1918, The History of the First World War*, Penquin Books

van Emden, R. and Humphries, S.(2003), *All Quiet on the Western Front,* Headline Book Publishing

van Emden, Richard. (2012), *Boy Soldiers of the Great War*, Bloomsbury Publishing plc

Newspapers & Periodicals, etc

Huddersfield Daily Examiner, (1914-1925), Trinity Mirror Group

Huddersfield Weekly Examiner, (1914-1919), Trinity Mirror Group

The Times, (1914-1919), Times Newspapers

Huddersfield Chronicle & West Yorkshire Advertiser, (1914-1916), Trinity Mirror Group

British Journal of Nursing, (1914-1919), MA Healthcare Ltd
Yorkshire Post, (1914-1919), Johnston Publishing Ltd
Yorkshire Evening Post, (1914-1919), Johnston Publishing Ltd
Leeds Mercury, (1914-1919), Yorkshire Post Newspapers Ltd
The Worker, (1914-1919)

Websites

http://www.britishpathe.com/video/huddersfield-presents-aeroplane-to-canada
www.britishpathe.com/video/king-george-v-queen-mary-visit-west-yorkshire
http://ww1centenary.oucs.ox.ac.uk/
http://issuu.com/the_blue_cross/docs/the_blue_cross_at_war

Index